Faith to Find a Job

Second Edition

by L.C. Brown-Bush

Faith to Find a Job

Faith to Find a Job

*To my precious **Mook, Mechoo, and Malia,***
...love you!
And to all of you who will mix your faith with the words of
faith and wisdom on these pages, this book is dedicated to you.

Faith to Find a Job

Table of Content

Introduction

Be Encouraged!

Nothing is Impossible with God!

Chapter 1 - From Fear to Faith ...1

Chapter 2 - Special Mercies for Job Hunters ...5

Chapter 3 - The Sower Sows the Word... the Resume ...9

Chapter 4 - The Power of Persistence ...13

Chapter 5 - Quality Seed... Employment Documents ...17

Chapter 6 - Job Search Anxiety ...21

Chapter 7 - God is Your Source ...27

Chapter 8 - Wisdom is the Principle Thing ...32

Chapter 9 - The Beauty of the Lord... Job Interviews ...40

Chapter 10 - Due Diligence ...47

Chapter 11 - God Gives the Increase ...54

Chapter 12 - Networking ...62

Chapter 13 - A First-Rate Resume ...70

Chapter 14 - Marketability... God's Plan ...84

Chapter 15 - The Realities of the Job Market ...90

Chapter 16 - The Favor of God ...95

Chapter 17 - I Believe... Therefore, I Speak ...102

Chapter 18 - God's Plan for Good Success ...109

Chapter 19 Divine Favor for the Humble ...117

Chapter 20 - The Supernatural... The Job Offer ...121

Conclusion - The Prayer of Prosperity

Faith to Find a Job

Prayer for Work

Return, O LORD!

How long?

And have compassion on Your servants.

Oh, satisfy us early with Your mercy,

That we may rejoice and be glad all our days!

Make us glad according to the days in which You have

afflicted us,

The years in which we have seen evil.

Let Your work appear to Your servants,

And Your glory to their children.

And let the beauty of the LORD our God be upon us,

And establish the work of our hands for us;

Yes, establish the work of our hands.

(Psalm 90:13-17)

Faith to Find a Job

Introduction

Be Encouraged!

Nothing is Impossible with God!

*Behold, My Servant, who I uphold, My Elect One in whom My
soul delights. He will not fail or be discouraged...
(Isaiah 42: 1 and 4)*

Faith is what we hold on to while we are waiting on a job
offer to manifest. If we are to be successful, our faith that a job
offer will come has to outweigh our fear that it will not. *My last
job search took ten months and my testimony is that I was never
discouraged.* The whole time I believed that God had a good job
for me, and that He would open the door to that opportunity
when the time was right.

Discouragement is the archenemy of the job hunter. It
makes the process of looking for a job much more painful than
it needs to be. After a series of disappointments,
discouragement can invade your soul. And if it gets the upper
hand, discouragement can convince you to give up and settle for
less than the best employment opportunity. So understand, my
testimony is that in spite of inconsistent results, periodic
rejections and a job hunt which went on longer than I first
imagined, I successfully dodged discouragement and pressed
into my job search until I connected to the *blessing* that God had
for me.

Faith to Find a Job

"...sanctify the Lord God in your hearts, and always be ready to give a defense to everyone who asks you a reason for the hope that is in you...." (I Peter 3: 15)

Looking back, I can see that there were three *pillars of strength* that supported my optimism about finding a job. First, I believed that I had high quality employment documents, and that I was conducting a first-rate job search. Second, I was realistic about the effort required, the time it might take to find a job, and the fact that rejection is an inevitable part of the process. I did not take rejection personally. In fact, when I met negative people, I countered their pessimism with *positive confessions of faith*. Finally, and without a doubt the most important reason I stayed encouraged, was that my confidence was not in me, the process of looking for a job, or reports about the economy. My confidence was *in God and* what the *Bible promised! My hope was up*...because it was rightly and safely invested in *The Almighty!*

This hope we have as an anchor of the soul, both sure and steadfast, and which enters the Presence behind the veil, (Hebrews 6:19)

One of the bed rocks of my faith were five wonderful words spoken by the Archangel that Stands in the Presence of God. The Gospel of Luke records the Angel Gabriel proclaiming, *"...nothing is **impossible** with **God**." (Luke 1:37) Search* the gospels, and you will find that Jesus said the same thing on more than one occasion. Moreover, that is where I started building

Faith to Find a Job

my *faith to find a job.* Before I sent out a single resume, I anchored those five words firmly into my spirit and came to this conclusion, "*All I need is a good job! I... might not be able to make it happen, but God can make it happen. Nothing is impossible with God. Indeed, blessing me with a good job is a small thing to God.*"

     Be encouraged! I have been a spirit-filled student of the Bible for more than twenty-five years. My prayers have been answered repeatedly because my prayer requests are rooted in what God promises to those who put their trust in Him. **Faith to Find a Job** is a pathway of encouragement and divine promise. In these pages, you will find realistic and practical advice that can help you conduct a successful job search. Moreover, you'll also find the building blocks of a faith that can conquer all your fears and support a hope that will sustain you until you connect to the employment blessing God has for you!

Be Blessed!

L.C. Brown Bush

Faith to Find a Job

Chapter 1

From Fear to Faith

"For whatever is born of God overcomes the world. And this is the victory that has overcome the world—our faith."
(1 John 5:4)

This book is about victorious faith but when it came to looking for employment, really **my testimony starts at the opposite end of the spectrum**. There was a time in my life when job hunting was something I dreaded. I did not think I was good at it. I feared that people would not like me, and I feared every type of discrimination possible. Still, like most people I had no choice, I needed to work. On this one occasion, I was having a hard time motivating myself to search for a job, because I did not think my effort would pay off! A battle was raging in my soul. I needed to move forward with my job search, but I was paralyzed by my own fears. Finally, I had enough, so I cried out to God.

*"This poor **man cried** out, and the **LORD** heard him, and saved him out of all his troubles."*
(Psalm 34:6)

Through tears, I cried out and told the Lord about my past experiences and the lack of results that made me feel like I did not have much of a chance. I honestly believed I would be a good employee, but the world was such a wicked and unfair place, *what chance did I have?* I laid out all my fears, and then the Lord spoke a calming word to my soul. His response to me was simply... *Goliath!*

Faith to Find a Job

I didn't hear that word audibly but Goliath was the essence of what the Lord spoke to my spirit, and by that I knew He was telling me that He was not impressed by what seemed like a giant dilemma to me. The Holy Spirit was saying, *"Trust me,"* and that divine word calmed my soul and helped me know that I was not in my problem alone.

Then God impressed me to hit the pavement, to go downtown and fill out employment applications. So that is what I did, and the fruit of my obedience was a job interview! More than that, however, I knew God had done it. So, from that time forward I understood that the Lord could open any door. I understood that He could and would provide for me. Faith was born. A positive attitude was born. Hope had decapitated my Goliath fears!

"And a champion went out from the camp of the Philistines, named Goliath, from Gath, whose height was six cubits and a span. Then he stood and cried out to the armies of Israel, and said to them, "Why have you come out to line up for battle? Am I not a Philistine, and you the servants of Saul? Choose a man for yourselves and let him come down to me. If he can fight with me and kill me, then we will be your servants. But if I prevail against him and kill him, then you shall be our servants and serve us. And the Philistine said, "I defy the armies of Israel this day; give me a man, that we may fight together." When Saul and all Israel heard these words of the Philistine, they were dismayed and greatly afraid" (I Samuel 17:4, 8-11)

The story of David and Goliath is just one of many that take us from fear to faith. At the beginning of this story, it's important to note that every soldier in the army was intimidated by Goliath. Everyone, even the King, was greatly afraid. They all had a duty to fight, but no one was willing to step up and face the giant. On some level, this scene parallels the common emotions that most of us fight when we are unemployed and facing the job market. Finding a job is an obligation that we have to live up to at some point in our life. However, on a personal level, when we are the one being challenged, it's easy to feel alone, inadequate and scared.

"No test...that comes your way is beyond the course of what others have had to face. All you need to remember is that God will never let you down; he'll never let you be pushed past your limit; he'll always be there to help you come through it."
(1 Corinthians 10:13 - The Message Bible)

Maybe you just finished school and ready or not, you have to find your first career position. Or perhaps after serving your company for more than ten or twenty years, you were unexpectedly laid off. Or possibly you've been looking for a job for more than a year, and its taking longer than you ever dreamed it would. These are daunting challenges that no one wants to face. Nevertheless, they are not beyond the course of what others have had to deal with, and they are not problems that are too big for God! If you are feeling lonely and inadequate about your job search skills consider this, *nobody likes looking for a job, and very few people are really good at it because it's something that most of us do only a few times in our life.*

The central goal of **Faith to Find a Job** is to encourage your faith for the entire job search journey...no matter how long it takes. The real key to your success is embracing the faith that God is with you in this battle. If you trust Him and

His promises, God will give you the victory. In fact, as David proclaimed just before he decapitated Goliath, this battle really belongs to the Lord.

> *"Then David said.., 'Let no man's heart fail because of him; your servant will go and fight with this Philistine.'"*

> *"Then David said to the Philistine... "This day the LORD will deliver you into my hand, and I will strike you and take your head from you. ...for the battle is the LORD's, and He will give you into our hands." (I Samuel 17:32, 45, 46 and 47)*

Reality Check: *The Lord is still in the business of empowering ordinary people to do extraordinary things!*

Suggested Bible Readings: You are in partnership with God Almighty... nothing is impossible for Him. If that is not your solid faith then maybe you need to start this faith journey by building your faith in God's ability to tower over the problems that are overwhelming you. The Bible stories in the list below can help build your faith in what God can do for, and through you. Read them and be encouraged!

Joseph's Promotion: Genesis 40:1 - 41:46; **Gideon and the Midianites:** Judges 6:1 - 7:25; **David and Goliath:** I Samuel 16; **Elisha and the Widow:** 2 Kings 4:1-7; **Jehoshaphat and the Invading Armies:** 2 Chronicles 20:1-25; **Daniel's Promotion:** Daniel 2:1-49 ; **Jesus Feeds Five Thousand:** John 6:1-15;

Chapter 2

Special Mercies for Job Hunters

*"For the kingdom of heaven is like a landowner who went out early in the morning to hire laborers for his vineyard. Now when he had agreed with the laborers for a denarius a day, he sent them into his vineyard. And he went out about the third hour and saw others standing idle in the marketplace, and said to them, 'You also go into the vineyard, and whatever is right I will give you.' So they went.   Again he went out about the sixth and the ninth hour, and did likewise. And about the eleventh hour he went out and found others standing idle, and said to them, 'Why have you been standing here idle all day?' They said to him, '**Because no one hired us**.' He said to them, 'You also go into the vineyard, and whatever is right you will receive.'*

*"So when evening had come, the owner of the vineyard said to his steward, 'Call the laborers and give them their wages, beginning with the last to the first.' And when those came who were hired about the eleventh hour, they each received a denarius. But when the first came, they supposed that they would receive more; and they likewise received each a denarius. And when they had received it, they complained against the landowner, saying, 'These last men have worked only one hour, and you made them equal to us who have borne the burden and the heat of the day.' But he answered one of them and said, 'Friend, I am doing you no wrong. Did you not agree with me for a denarius? Take what is yours and go your way. I wish to give to this last man the same as to you. Is it not lawful for me to do what I wish with my own things? Or is your eye evil because **I am good?**' So the last will be first, and the first last. For many are called, but few chosen." (Matthew 20: 1-16)*

In reading the verse of scripture quoted here, it is easy to imagine that the landowner and his extraordinary generosity is a type and reflection of God. The most common interpretation of this parable relates to the eternal reward for our faith in Jesus Christ. It doesn't matter how long you've believed, or whether you've labored for the kingdom or not, Heaven will be equally sweet for all believers.

Still, I think this parable holds a unique meaning for those who are struggling with the dilemma of joblessness. I believe it reveals God's special mercy and grace for those who are unemployed and under-employed. That's how I see it because there was a time when the pain of not having a job pierced my soul. My family members and most people I knew had good jobs, regular income, and the peace of mind that their financial needs would be addressed. They didn't know what I was going through, and I was a bit perplexed myself. I had been a believer for years and a faithful tither. I had served the Lord with my Christian witness, but at that moment I felt like those laborers who were not hired until the eleventh hour. I had bills to pay and a child to support. I wanted to work... but I was at home idle because *no one had hired me!*

Then the Holy Spirit revealed to me that those men who had worked all day long had received more. All day long they had enjoyed the peace of mind that came with knowing that their family would eat dinner that night and their financial needs would be addressed. The landowner was not being arbitrarily generous, he was being compassionate and merciful. The Holy Spirit showed me that the landowner was sensitive to the fact that those men who had only labored a few hours, also had needs and love ones depending on them. The gift of a full day's wage was *a quality gift*...a blessing sufficient to meet their needs. That is a type and reflection of the God we serve. That... is God's heart for the unemployed, the under-employed and those who bring their needs to Him and seek His provision.

> *"....when they had received it, they complained against the landowner, saying, 'These last men have worked only one hour, and you made them equal to us who have borne the burden and the heat of the day.'" (Matthew 20:11-12)*

All the laborers received a full day's wage but most of them had not earned it. It does not seem right. It does not seem fair. It is lavishly generous, uncommon...divine! Yet, this parable speaks to one of the biggest hindrances to our faith...our sense of unworthiness. When most of us look into the mirror, we don't see a man or women worthy of a blessing. When we look in the mirror, we see the fact that we've neglected our faith and haven't put forth our best effort in life...or in looking for a job. *So why should God bless us?*

> *"...is your eye evil because **I am good?**'" (Matthew 20:15)*

This parable that Jesus gave us, illustrates that God's mercy does not flow out of our goodness, it flows out of ...*His goodness*. Look at the parable again, the landowner is the lead actor and hero of this story. We see him moving and we see the motivation of his heart revealed. We don't know anything about the laborers, whether they are good or evil. Nevertheless, the landowner is not picking and choosing which one to bless. No, we see him providing adequately for all those he encounters. We see him living out what Jesus said about our Heavenly Father in Matthew 5:45, *"...your Father in heaven; ...makes His sun rise on the evil and on the good, and sends rain on the just and on the unjust."*

Faith to Find a Job

None of us, no matter how good we look on the outside, is worthy of God's blessing. Those of us who are blessed, understand that the grace of the Cross covers our sins and insufficiencies. The grace of the Cross redeems us from the curse of the law that our works deserve...*the curse of poverty, sickness and death.* (Galatians 3:13-14)

The Lord is not interested in your past sin as much as He cares about having an encounter with you. God has special mercies for the unemployed and under-employed that has everything to do with His kindness and nothing to do with your worthiness. Carry your sins to the Cross and believe in your redemption from the curse! God is good and lavishly generous, and He has provisions and special mercies for those he encounters in prayer!

Reality Check: What a wonderful and generous God we serve. God's grace is the good news of the Gospel. For God loved the world so much that he sent his Son to die the death that we deserve, so we can live the blessed life that Jesus deserves. The love that the Father poured out on us through the His son's death on the Cross is lavishly generous, uncommon...divine! And we need to understand, the ultimate sacrifice has been made for us, not because we are good...but because God is good. **If you have not accepted Jesus Christ as your Lord and Savior...do it today!**

Faith to Find a Job

Chapter 3

The Sower Sows the Word... the Resume

*"Listen! Behold, a sower went out to sow. And it happened, as he sowed, that some seed fell by the wayside; and the birds of the air came and devoured it. Some fell on stony ground, where it did not have much earth; and immediately it sprang up because it had no depth of earth. But when the sun was up it was scorched, and because it had no root it withered away. And some seed fell among thorns; and the thorns grew up and choked it, and it yielded no crop. But **other seed fell on good ground and yielded a crop that sprang up, increased and produced**: some thirtyfold, some sixty, and some a hundred." And He said to them, "He who has ears to hear, let him hear!"(Mark 4:3-9)*

The Holy Spirit impressed me to write down exactly what I wanted in my next job. So I did. I wanted a job with a specific job title. I wanted to work for a large organization downtown. I wanted my own office and a specific salary, and no less. And finally, I did not want to be pressured into a commitment to work overtime. Availability for overtime is a topic that usually comes up in job interviews, but I needed a regular schedule because I had a small child and a disabled mother that needed me at home in the evenings.

In any case, then the Lord led me to submit my resume unsolicited to about 40 firms downtown. That was a God idea inspired by the *Parable of the Sower* because up until that time, answering job posting or being referred by an employment agency was the only way I knew to look for a position. However, this experience taught me something new. Within three weeks, I had accepted an offer for a job that was in all points an answer to my specific prayer. The Lord had helped me tap into the hidden job market that I had heard was out there, but up until that time, had no idea how to find. It turns out that my application showed up just about the time an opening came up at the firm, so they called me in for an interview. Right away they saw that I had the qualifications they were looking for, so they hired me. The firm saved the time and expense of posting the position and fielding through a stack of resumes and candidates. And from my perspective, *I had no competition* for the job. *It was a Divine connection.*

The *Parable of the Sower* holds promise for job hunters. It is the spiritual framework for the whole of our endeavor because it promises a harvest for our diligent efforts. I remember listening to one young man (who was not particularly spiritual) talk about his job-hunting efforts. His attitude was so positive, and he had faith that he was putting forth a sustained realistic effort to find a job. He had sowed bountifully, I could see that, so I told him confidently and in faith, *"then you'll get a job."* Shortly after that proclamation his harvest came in, not because I am a prophet but because the Word works, and I believe it.

On the other hand, I remember counseling a young woman who was grappling with poverty and hoping to get a job from a single application she submitted over a year prior to our conversation. She had always wanted to work for the city's transit department, and she was believing, I feared *in vain,* for a harvest from that single application. Through the *Parable of the Sower*, I encouraged her to do more to find a job. And later, I also prayed that God would give her wisdom and light, so she could see the error of her ways.

> *'But this I say: He who sows sparingly will also reap sparingly, and **he who sows bountifully will also reap bountifully.**"*
> *(2 Corinthians 9:6)*

Faith to Find a Job

Listen, one or two grass seeds will not produce a lawn, and when it comes to job hunting, some seed (applications) will fall by the wayside (the waste basket). Some will fall on stony ground (you may get a phone interview, that's all). Some will fall among the thorns (you may go all the way through the interview process but the competition will eventually choke out the opportunity). However, some will fall on good ground and produce (a job offer). Let me encourage you to let the spiritual principle of sowing and reaping frame your faith and efforts to find a job. Meditate the scriptures in this book that promise an expected end and let the principle of sowing and reaping generously, frame your faith. Then, I can tell you confidently and in faith that one of your applications will fall on good ground and produced a job offer. I believe that!

Tap into the Hidden Job Market. Thanks to the Internet it is easier than ever to tap into the hidden job market. By that I mean, those employment opportunities that are not listed with agencies or job banks. These days many companies are listing job opportunities exclusively on their company websites, so you will need to do some research, but by going directly to the company site you may encounter less competition for your dream job.

Get organized and develop a list of organizations and websites to explore. Use Google search, major business communications, or other published resources to find organizations that hire people with your qualifications. Additionally, search the job sites of large corporations, banks, hotels, hospitals, law firms, colleges, and universities. Also, search government job sites like USA.gov or state and municipal job sites. Be resourceful and think about the type of organizations that can use someone with your knowledge and job skills.

Submit your applications thoughtfully and revisit websites periodically. The first few times you review a company's job postings you may not see a position that interests you or matches your qualifications. However, be patient and from time to time go back and review posting on those sites. If you're persistent, in time a job will open that's right for you.

Reality Check: *One or two grass seeds will not produce a lawn. It is an uncommon experience to find a good job by submitting one or a few applications. So make a commitment to plant ('sow") job applications and resumes in an abundance. Dig deep...and tap into the hidden job market.*

Chapter 4

The Power of Persistence

"Then He spoke a parable to them, that men always ought to pray and not lose heart..." (Luke 18:1)

The Lord has given us two very inspiring parables on the power of persistence. The first, found in Luke 11:5-9 is the story of two friends who happen to be neighbors. One friend asks a favor of the other at a very inopportune time. In the middle of the night he fervently knocks at his neighbor's door with a need. However, his friend, tired and sleepy hollers back, *"Go away, my family and I are in bed. Come back in the morning and I'll help you then."* But his friend won't listen because he has an immediate need, so he keeps pounding and pounding at his neighbor's door until his neighbor gets up and gives him what he needs.

The other parable, found in Luke 18:1-7, is about a persistent widow and an unjust judge. The judge grants the widow's petition for no other reason, than that the widow is persistent. I'd better give her what she wants, he reasons, because I can see she is going to worry me until she gets what she is after. No matter how you see God...as a preoccupied friend or as an indifferent judge, Jesus is telling us through these parables that we always ought to pray and not lose heart.. because if we persist, we'll get what we're after.

Faith to Find a Job

In the last chapter, we discussed how important it is to sow job applications and resumes in abundance if we want to reap the abundant harvest of a job offer! In this chapter, we'll look at the power of persistence as a strategy for sowing abundantly for a job. I've seen this strategy work effectively for several people who persisted until they got jobs at the companies of their choice. One young man, a certified diesel mechanic, identified a company that he heard paid well and that had a large fleet of trucks. So he decided to stop by one day to see if they were hiring. He talked to the receptionist in the lobby, and on the way out he walked around to the garage, and spoke to the hiring manager. Both confirmed that the company wasn't hiring at the time but they both told him to try back. A little over a month passed, and he stopped in again, He talked to the receptionist, and then to the hiring manager in the garage, but still they told him the company wasn't hiring mechanics. A month or so later, he stopped by again...but still no luck.

Over the course of a year, maybe a little longer, he stopped by numerous times to see if a mechanic position had opened up. Then one day he stopped in and the receptionist who knew his name by then, greeted him with a big smile, a job application and news that the company was looking for a diesel mechanic. The hiring manager also seemed pleased to setup a job interview. At that point, it was merely a formality *...of course he got the job.*

Sometime later I heard of a younger man who used the same strategy to get a job close to home. He identified the place that he wanted to work, and then he kept going back until he got a job there.

Faith to Find a Job

Listen, persistence says to a potential employer, I am really interested. I appreciate this company. I am a motivated worker. I am reliable. *Persistence carves out an advantage* over other job candidates, because it says I've worked harder than anyone else for this opportunity.

Finally, know that you don't have to sow your persistent seeds in person. Some years ago, when I was working in a Human Resources department, I saw the power of persistence work for an applicant who over the course of a year continued to submit his resume for similar job opportunities in the computer field. It seemed like once a week we got a resume from this man with a unique sounding East Indian name, until finally he was called in for an interview *...which led to a job offer.*

"Ask and it will be given to you; seek and you will find; knock and the door will be opened to you. For everyone who asks receives; he who seeks finds; and to him who knocks, the door will be opened." (Luke 11:9-10)

Understand that on several levels those who are job hunting *by faith* will need to cultivate the virtue of persistence: in prayer, in faith, and in the practical aspects of their job search. Persistence, like sowing and reaping, is a spiritual principle that promises a harvest (a job offer). Indeed, I believe the Lord is telling us through these parables that we always ought to **persist...**because if we do...**we'll eventually get what we're after... a job.**

Reality Check: *Persistence carves out an advantage over other job candidates, because it says I've worked harder than anyone else for this opportunity.*

Faith to Find a Job

Suggested Bible Reading: Parables of Persistence: Luke 11:5-9 and Luke 18: 1-7

Chapter 5

Quality Seed... Employment Documents

"To whom much is given, much is required." *(Luke 12:48)*

In doing the research for this book, I came across a bit of applied agricultural science that I thought illustrated a vital principle for job seekers. I found out that *seed quality* is inextricably tied to yield. *In cold unfavorable climates, seed of inferior quality may fail to produce a crop. High quality seed*, on the other hand, *will produce a crop in spite of poor weather conditions.*

In a tight job market, you cannot afford to sow sloppy or incomplete applications or a poorly constructed resume. The quality of your employment documents, a potential employer may very well conclude, indicate the quality of the work product you are likely to produce for their company. If you have spelling errors in your resume or cover letter, a potential employer might conclude that you'll have spelling errors in your work product. If you turn in a sloppy incomplete job application, that may convey to a would be employer that you will turn in sloppy incomplete work. So understand, it's vital that you do your best work when formulating the documents that you use to search for a job.

Following are a *few* general tips to help you turn in excellent quality work when sowing your resumes *and job applications* in an unfavorable job market.

➢ ***Don't job hunt when you're tired.*** Specifically, don't start an on-line job application when you're fatigued. Wait until you are rested and alert so you can submit complete job applications that contain correct complete information that you feel good about.

➢ ***Work smarter by developing an employment data sheet.*** An employment data sheet should contain all the details you might be asked on a job application. It should include specific information related to your employment history including dates, company names, addresses, phone numbers, names of your supervisors, salary information, etc. It should also include details related to your educational background and the names and contact information for personal and professional references. Verify the spelling and accuracy of the information that's on your data sheet. Then always...***always*** *have it with you when you're filling out a job application on-line or in person. Using an employment data sheet is the smart way to work.* If all the detail you need to complete your job application is on your data sheet, then all you'll have to do is copy the information from your data sheet to the job application in a neat and accurate way.

➢ ***Look at resume and cover letter books to get ideas and strategies for developing your employment documents.*** *After prayer*, I start every job search at the library or online reviewing resume and cover letter samples. Many samples are written by hiring managers and successful career counselors who share their perspective of the employment documents that they consider to be effective. These books are also full of inspiration and job search strategies. Many of them are arranged by job category so it is also possible to find *descriptive language* that you can use in your own employment documents.

➢ ***Modify your resume with some of the same words that are in the job posting that you are responding to.*** A customized resume will demonstrate that your qualifications are on target.

➢ ***Use spell check and grammar check before you finalize your documents and if possible, submit them in PDF format.*** Don't skip this important step, especially if you are submitting a word processing document online. Word processing programs are designed to highlight spelling and grammar inconsistencies, so understand your spelling and grammar mistakes will pop out if you submit your document in Word format. That is also why it is important that you resolve all spelling and grammar issues before you submit your employment documents, and if possible, submit them in PDF format.

➢ ***Ask someone to proofread your employment documents.*** If you can afford it, use a resume service to help you pull together your employment documents. A good job is worth the investment. If you cannot afford one of these services, ask someone who has communication skills that you respect to proofread your documents. If you cannot find anyone you trust to proofread your employment documents, then use the *Read Aloud* feature on your computer, and have your computer read your documents back to you. The point is, even if you have a good command of the English language, and you have proofread your documents carefully, it is still possible to miss mistakes in documents you develop yourself. So, do not be overly confident or sensitive, but seek out and incorporate suggestions that will improve your resume and cover letters.

Trust in the LORD with all your heart,
And lean not on your own understanding;
In all your ways acknowledge Him,
And He shall direct your paths. (Proverbs 3: 5-6)

Finally, understand that high quality effective employment documents are the ***fruit of prayer***. Pray and ask the Lord to help you to do your best work when job hunting and to give you the resume and cover letter that you need to get the position that He has in store for you. Acknowledge God in this ...and He will direct your path!

Reality Check: *Do something excellent for yourself. Develop employment documents that make you look good as a job applicant. A high-quality resume will produce results ...even in an unfavorable job market.*

Faith to Find a Job

Chapter 6

Job Search Anxiety

"Therefore, do not worry and be anxious, saying, What are we going to have to eat? or, What are we going to have to drink? or, What are we going to have to wear?

For the Gentiles wish for and crave and diligently seek all these things, and your heavenly Father knows well that you need them all.

*But seek (aim at and strive after) first of all His kingdom and His righteousness (**His way of doing and being right),** and then all these things taken together will be given you besides."*
(Matthew 6:31-34- Amplified Bible)

Faith to Find a Job is a winning approach to searching for employment, but it's not rooted in a good idea, a twelve-step program, or a slick new coaching plan. The simple truth is, this book is about encouraging you to seek God in your endeavor to find work. Walking by faith is a time honored approach to living that is rooted in the belief that the guidance and wisdom of the Holy Spirit is all you need to produce victory in your life.

*"I know your works. See, **I have set before you an open door, and no one can shut it**; for you have a little strength, have kept My word, and have not denied My name.*
(Revelation 3:8)

God is bigger than any problem. He can open any door! No one can shut the doors that God opens for us. On our own, we can't open the door for ourselves, but the Apostle Paul summed up the power that our faith in God adds to any situation when he said, *"I can do all things through Christ, who strengthens me!"*

Paul was saying, through the Lord's teaching... through his wisdom... through His way of doing and being right, he found the strength and ability to do anything he needed to do. In the same way, we can find the strength and ability to do all things. Through the Lord's way of doing and being right we can find a good job. That, and only that, sums up the winning approach in this book.

"Therefore, do not worry and be anxious, saying, What are we going to have to eat? or, What are we going to have to drink? or, What are we going to have to wear?"
(Matthew 6:31-Amplified Bible)

Matthew 6:31 drives home the point that God gave us a biblical doctrine to address the realistic aspects of our lives. In this verse of scripture Jesus is talking to people who were worried about practical things. How are we going to eat? What are we going to wear? How are we going to pay our bills? Many of those people were like many of us, living payday-to-payday and moment-to-moment. Like some of us, some of them were anxious and stressed because they were in crisis mode or one or two paychecks away from a crisis.

I remember being there. My substitute teaching job had run out for the summer, my money was almost gone, and after a month of sending out resumes *in faith*, I hadn't received a single response. Something was wrong and I had good reasons to be anxious and stressed, but I knew what to do. I got quiet and prayed, and that was my posture *for hours...for days...for weeks!*

"The young lions lack and suffer hunger; but those who **seek** *the* **LORD** *shall not lack any* **good thing***."* **(Psalm 34:10**)

Talk about high anxiety! I was in crisis mode but prayer brought me through. The fruit of seeking the Lord and spending that time on my knees was a retail sales position that filled in the financial gaps until something better came along, a new more effective resume that produced results in a matter of days, and a faith that kept me encouraged until I accepted a good paying full-time job that more than covered my needs. Psalm 34:10 says that *those who seek the Lord shall not lack any good thing.* I trust those words and that's why I pray.

"Be anxious for nothing, but *in everything* **by prayer** *and supplication, with thanksgiving, let your requests be made known to God; and the peace of God, which surpasses all understanding, will guard your hearts and minds through Christ Jesus." (Philippians 4:6-7)*

Be anxious for nothing, but.... Do you see it? Do you see that the Word is telling us that *anxiety* is God's call to prayer. Unfortunately it is also the devil's call to bury our heads in the sand! The fruit of prayer is a peace that will guard your heart and mind and wisdom that will lead you to realistic solutions. Trying to forget your problems by watching hours of television, using drugs or alcohol or even hanging out with your friends, may relieve some of your stress for a while, but none of those worldly medications will make your problems go away. In fact, if that is the only way you deal with your problems, you may end up wasting valuable time and making matters even worse.

Faith to Find a Job

"Then the kingdom of heaven shall be likened to ten virgins who took their lamps and went out to meet the bridegroom. Now five of them were wise, and five were foolish. Those who were foolish took their lamps and took no oil with them but the wise took oil in their vessels with their lamps." (Matthew 25: 1-4)

Managing Job Search Anxiety

Job search anxiety is usually associated with a financial crisis that is the results of a diminishing income. If you're facing a crisis or on the brink of one, first remember that your anxiety is a call to prayer and faith. So pray and ask God for wisdom and then act wisely. Additionally, if you adhere to the following wise suggestions you may be able to avoid job search anxiety altogether:

> ➤ *Understand, it may take a while to connect to a really good job.* One of the reasons I experienced a money crunch, was because I assumed my job search would only last a few weeks. *(Because as I wrote in an earlier chapter, my previous job search for a career position only took a few weeks.)* Nonetheless, it was a mistake to gauge my current job search on my past experience. Each job search is different, because you and/or the economy may be different. Additionally, it could be that the focus of your last job search was an entry level position, whereas now you're looking for a more senior position. Now, you may believe you are overqualified for the majority of the jobs in your field, which means it could take longer to connect to the level of position you are currently searching for.

Faith to Find a Job

In reviewing various statistics related to the length of the average job search, three to six months seems like a good estimate of how long it can take. However, about a year prior to my last job search, I read an article which indicated that following a layoff, the average job search for individuals with career experience was about 18 months. That was how long it was taking individuals with advanced career experience to find positions comparable to the one lost as a consequence of a layoff. In any case, once I realized that I wasn't going to connect to the perfect job as quickly as I had in the past, I bought into the 18 month projection and found a second job to fill in the financial gaps. Additionally, I conducted my financial affairs with more wisdom when I realized it might take longer than a year to find a good career position.

➢ *If you're unemployed and facing serious financial difficulties, you may need to conduct **a dual job search**. One for a job to help address your immediate needs and the other for a long-term career position.* If you have serious financial needs, pray and then find a job...*any job*. However, once you've connected, don't settle for being *under employed,* keep looking for God's best job for you. Between my substitute teaching job and a retail sales position, I was able to cover my expenses while I actively looked for a full time career position. I was grateful for those jobs that put money in my pocket and helped me pay my bills, but I knew they were not God's best. So I kept looking until I found a full-time permanent position that more than covered my needs.

Faith to Find a Job

*The ravens brought him bread and meat in the morning, and bread and meat in the evening; and he drank from the brook. And **it happened after a while that the brook dried up**, because there had been no rain in the land. (I Kings 17:6-7)*

__Reality Check:__ A financial crisis can be a scary time but the Lord can use it to move you in to your next assignment. If your resources dry up, understand that God still loves you and has not forsaken you, nor are you being punished or counted unworthy of a blessing. Seek the Lord and walk in wisdom and God will guide you to your next provision.

Faith to Find a Job

Chapter 7

God is Your Source

"So Abraham rose early in the morning, and took bread and a skin of water; and putting it on her shoulder, he gave it and the boy to Hagar, and sent her away. Then she departed and wandered in the Wilderness of Beersheba. And the water in the skin was used up, and she placed the boy under one of the shrubs. Then she went and sat down across from him at a distance of about a bowshot; for she said to herself, "Let me not see the death of the boy." So she sat opposite him, and lifted her voice and wept.

And God heard the voice of the lad. Then the angel of God called to Hagar out of heaven, and said to her, "What ails you, Hagar? Fear not, for God has heard the voice of the lad where he is. Arise, lift up the lad and hold him with your hand, for I will make him a great nation."

Then God opened her eyes, and she saw a well of water. *And she went and filled the skin with water, and gave the lad a drink. So God was with the lad; and he grew and dwelt in the wilderness, and became an archer. He dwelt in the Wilderness of Paran; and his mother took a wife for him from the land of Egypt." (Genesis 21: 14-21)*

Without notice Hagar was *fired* and sent away into the wilderness with nothing more than *bread and a skin of water* to sustain her and her son. I can imagine that she was scared, angry and perhaps, somewhat remorseful. Then her meager provisions ran out, and she found herself immersed in a crisis that she didn't even author. She thought her son was going to die, but then God showed up with a promise of life and a miracle provision in answer to prayer.

An involuntary termination, even a lay-off, is almost always a bitter pill to swallow. It doesn't matter if your co-workers took you out for a farewell lunch and your company gave you what they considered to be a generous severance package, once you're unemployed you can still find yourself wrestling with fear, resentment and a sense that your years of dedication and hard work were all for nothing. Add to that, the panic you might feel because you have a mortgage to pay, a family to support and an unemployment check that only covers a fraction of your expenses. You want to work. You want to fix the situation but finding the type of job you need ...well, it is going to take time!

I remember a day recently after my divorce when a similar situation had me panicked and in tears. I was cleaning the house, crying and trying to figure out what I was going to do when the Holy Spirit said to me, *"Why are you crying, haven't I always taken care of you?"*

When I heard those words in my spirit, I was a bit astounded. So much so that I stopped crying and immediately began thinking about what the Lord had just said. Honestly, until that moment I had not seen God as my source. My mother had always taken care of me. My family ...my job, those things were truly what I thought had supported me all my life. Then, without hearing another word from the Holy Spirit, I began to receive the fullness of what the Lord was telling me. Whether I knew it or not, all my life God had provided for me. He was the source of every resource that had taken care of my needs. Yes, I was in a tight spot and in need of a new resource, but God had not changed. He was still willing to provide for me, but He was calling me up to a higher faith. The time had come for me to learn how to go directly to God for my provision, to start trusting in the Source and not the resources.

> *" Cursed is the man who trusts in man*
> *And makes flesh his strength,*
> *Whose heart departs from the LORD.*
> *Blessed is the man who trusts in the LORD,*
> *And whose hope is the LORD. (Jeremiah 17:5 and 7)*

Are you angry ...panicked? If so, *why?* Your former employer is not your God! Whether you realize it or not, God is your source and has always been your source. God gave you the job that you lost, and He can give you another job... better than the best job you ever had. God is still willing to provide for you, but He is also calling you to a higher faith. It's time that you learn how to go directly to the Source...to trust God for your provision.

*Pursue peace with all people, and holiness, without which no one will see the Lord: looking carefully **lest anyone fall short of the grace of God; lest any root of bitterness springing up cause trouble** (Hebrew 12: 14-15)*

If you feel victimized by the circumstances surrounding a job loss, understand that your recovery starts by trusting God's word. Anger is spiritual blindness (1 John 2:10-11) and bitterness is incompatible with the grace of God (*Hebrew 12: 14-15*). The answers to our prayers are hindered by the lack of forgiveness in our hearts (Mark 11:24-26). So, you cannot afford *not* to forgive. As hard as it may seem, forgiving, trusting God for justice (Psalm 103:6) and moving pass the hurtful circumstances are *God's way of doing and being right.* And remember God's way of doing and being right is connected to His provision (Matthew 6:31-34- Amplified Bible).

Faith to Find a Job

"Assuredly, I say to you, no prophet is accepted in his own country. So all those in the synagogue, when they heard these things, were filled with wrath, and rose up and thrust Him out of the city; and they led Him to the brow of the hill on which their city was built, that they might throw Him down over the cliff. Then passing through the midst of them, He went His way.
(Luke 4: 24 and 28-30)

Jesus understood the pain of rejection, but he also understood the power of walking in love. He knew that as he walked in love toward his fellow man, God would empower Him to succeed. So, Jesus did not allow the types of offenses that cripple most of us to penetrate His soul. He understood that anger and bitterness were incompatible with the Holy Spirit, whereas love and peace attract God's divine presence. In the passage of scripture quoted just above, we read about Jesus being rejected by the people in his town. They were so mad at him that they thrust him out of the city and attempted to kill him...and yet he passed through the midst of them and went His way. *It was a supernatural escape* made possible only by God!

Most of us (if we were lucky enough to escape the crowd) would be wounded by that one traumatic event for the rest of our lives. We would replay the horrible scene over and over again in our minds and we would tell God and anybody else that would hear us how unfair we had been treated. And yet not long *after* actually walking through this experience Jesus taught, *"love your enemies, bless those who curse you, do good to those who hate you, and pray for those who spitefully use you and persecute you, that you may be sons of your Father in heaven."* *(Matthew5:44-45).* When we suffer for righteousness sake, Jesus taught, it is an indication that we have a great heavenly reward (Matthew 5:12). And if we trust God for our justice and refuse to repay evil for evil, we may inherit a blessing (I Peter 3:8-9).

> *These things I have spoken to you, that in Me you may have peace. In the **world** you will have tribulation; but be of good cheer, I have **overcome** the **world**." (John 16:33)*

Reality Check: Unlike most of us, Jesus didn't worship his wounds he overcame them. In fact, he displayed the height of strength when he cried out from the Cross... 'Father forgive them, for they know not what they do!' When we learn to trust God for justice, forgive and move beyond our pain, we will reconnect to the joy of the Lord and the Source of our provisions and blessings. If you're having a hard time forgiving someone who hurt you, pray with sincerity this simple prayer:

> *"God I want to forgive this person that hurt me, but I can't do it on my own. So if you will take away my bitterness and pain, I will agree to let it go... and I will forgive them!"*

Faith to Find a Job

Chapter 8

Wisdom is the Principle Thing

"For by wise counsel you can wage your war, and in an abundance of counselors there is victory and safety."
(Proverbs 24:6 - Amplified Bible)

I remember being in the middle of my last job search, working as a substitute teacher during the day and at a department store on the weekends. I had gone on a few job interviews, and I was feeling like it was only a matter of time before I would connect to a really good paying position. Then one day I was talking to a fellow sales associate who told me her husband was also looking for a professional job. He had a business degree and had held a very responsible position in management when he got involved in a union conflict that resulted in his forced resignation. At the time, he was driving a cab and working with *head hunters* in an effort to find another professional position. Nonetheless, his wife told me that he was growing increasingly discouraged because he didn't feel as though his job search was *really* going anywhere.

So I offered a few suggestions and shared some of what I thought was working for me. Throughout the course of the conversation, however, I discovered that my friend's husband didn't know how to use the Internet *to search for a job.* This woman had described an intelligent, competent... accomplished professional...but he didn't really know how to look for a job. And he wasn't the only one, many of the ladies that I met at that department store longed to secure better positions, but the majority of them did not have a resume and most of them felt that they weren't really qualified to do anything else but work at that store. I met people who were hoping to improve their lot in life by finding a better job, but they knew it was doubtful, because they weren't looking for a better job.

"My people are destroyed for lack of knowledge." (Hosea 4:6)

Many people don't know how to look for a job. They don't have a resume. They don't think they have anything to offer! They're underemployed because the only jobs that are assessable to them, are jobs that don't require anything more than a job application. Or they're underemployed, because they've convinced themselves that the job market is too tight, and they're either overqualified or under-qualified for the type of job they really want. Some of these people are working two jobs and double shifts just to make ends meet, but even with all that...ends don't meet.

*"Wisdom is the principal thing; Therefore get wisdom. And in **all your getting**, get understanding." **(Proverbs 4:7**)*

Listen, you cannot find a job if you are not looking for one. And if you don't know how to conduct a job search *be honest with yourself,* and then sit down and make a plan to increase your knowledge in this area.

The knowledge you need is everywhere and in many cases it's free. All you have to do is go after it! And understand, you will heighten your *faith to find a job,* if you know that you have a first-rate resume and a winning strategy to find a good job.

Faith to Find a Job

Remember I told you earlier how I prayed a specific prayer, mailed off my resume and found the job I prayed for in one month. Well, let's fast forward a bit... my next job hunt was several years later. I was older and I had not held a career position in almost **seven years!** Like a lot of women, binding family obligations had caused me to suspend my career for a few years, but then the day came when those obligations dissipated, and I wanted ...*needed* to re-enter the job market in order to find a good paying career position.

When the time came however, everything about job hunting had changed. I had changed ...and the resume that had helped me snag a great job when I was in my thirties, was dating me as being in my forties ...and outdating my experience. It was really spooky for a while, sending out resumes in faith and getting absolutely no response. I knew something was wrong and my gut instinct told me that the problem was my resume. So *I cried out to God and asked Him to give me the resume I needed to get the job that He had in store for me.* Then I got off my knees and went to the library...***again!***

Where there is no counsel, the people fall; But in the **multitude** *of* **counselors** *there is safety.* **(Proverbs 11:14**)

In my opinion, *after prayer*, every job search should start at the library, even if you think you know what you are doing ...even if you have conducted successful job searches in the past, it is only wise to update your resume and refresh your job hunting skills.

I started my last job search at the library, but at first I just reviewed resume and cover letter books because I wanted to *refresh the style and content of my employment documents.* However, after sowing my resume in faith, and getting no responses, I returned to the library because *I wanted to learn strategies* for re-entering the job market after a substantial hiatus, and I knew that type of scenario was addressed in those career development books that I had used as a style guide.

*My brethren, count it all joy when you fall into various trials, knowing that the testing of your faith produces patience. But let patience have its perfect work, that you may be perfect and complete, lacking nothing. **If any of you lacks wisdom, let him ask of God, who gives to all liberally and without reproach, and it will be given to him**. (James 1: 2-5)*

I *restarted* my job search by going back to the library to *look for strategies* to address the problems with my resume. The first thing that impacted me was the countless resumes that did not have dates associated with the educational credentials. More than anything else, I felt the dates associated with my college education revealed my age. In truth, I didn't mind people meeting me and knowing my age, because I knew I was very young looking, but I didn't want anyone conjuring up an image of what I might be like based on my age. So immediately, I decided to remove the dates associated with my educational credentials.

Removing the date that I received my bachelor's degree resolved the age discrimination issue, but there was still a huge time gap between the present and my last career position. So I kept searching for strategies that would help me deal with gaps in work history. Interestingly enough, most of the books that addressed issues related to *job experience*, advised that a resume only cover the most recent, relevant experience going back no further than ten years. The more I researched, however, the more I began to understand that an effective resume is not a chronological summary of an individual's job history. An effective resume...is a *sales tool*.

I went on to read about women who had suspended their careers to raise their family and later successfully re-entered the job market by promoting past work experience or even volunteer experience gained working in their communities. However, then I spotted a resume that turned out to be my bulls-eye solution. It was a functional resume....*with no dates!* It was such a bold approach... but *I loved it!*

So, I reworked the style of my resume ...and removed all the dates. Then I *posted* my resume again on the major job sites and my phone began to ring. Within a week, I had an interview at an employment agency...that led to an interview at a well-respected law firm. From that point on my job search took off. I was fielding phone calls frequently and interviewing every several weeks. And like I said at the beginning of this Chapter, I had come to believe that it was only a matter of time before God would open a door with a job offer.

*Therefore **judge nothing before the time**, until the Lord comes, who will both bring to light the hidden things of darkness and reveal the counsels of the hearts. Then each one's praise will come from God. (1 Corinthians 4:5)*

Understand, my strategy was not to hide my age or the age of my job experience. My strategy was to get my foot in the door to interview. I wanted potential employers to meet me and hear me talk about my qualifications. In the first few minutes of every interview, *everyone asked about the dates on my resume, why they weren't there.* That gave me a chance to explain the special circumstances that led me to suspend my career. And it also gave me an opportunity to explain why I was currently available to dedicate myself to developing a new career. After I explained my unique resume, the rest of the job interview was about my qualifications and why I thought I was the right person for the job.

Obviously, I didn't get every job I interviewed for, but the fact that potential employers were interested in me fed my faith. And more often than not, I left my interviews believing that it went well, and that I had a good chance of getting the job. That fed my faith even more.

Get Honest ...Get Organized ...Get Understanding

"...the path of the just is like the shining sun, that shines ever brighter unto the perfect day. The way of the wicked is like darkness, they do not know what makes them stumble. My son, give attention to my words; incline your ear to my sayings. Do not let them depart from your eyes, keep them in the midst of your heart. For they are life to those who find them, and health to all their flesh. " (Proverbs 4: 18-22)

Get honest and get organized by sitting down and making a list of what you think you need to resurrect or revitalize your job search. If you need to spend time learning how to find a job then turn off the television, go to your local library, search the web, and spend time learning what you need to do in order to turn your job search around. Understand however, it is not going to happen overnight. Your goal is to improve your *jobhunting skills* by learning from books and professionals that you believe have knowledge that can help you.

In organizing your job search, think about the following list, and what you might specifically need to find a good job. Do you need:

> ➢ to improve or refresh your job hunting skills,
> ➢ a better resume and cover letters,
> ➢ strategies to address employment gaps, getting fired, etc.
> ➢ a computer to search for jobs on the internet,
> ➢ marketability and better job skills,
> ➢ clothes to wear on an interview,
> ➢ transportation to the interview or a place of employment,
> ➢ a telephone where potential employers can contact you or leave a message.

The first four items on this list can all be obtained at your local library. If you're unemployed, plan to get up tomorrow and spend the next several days at the library learning how to search for a job. If you're underemployed, then plan to spend your next several off days at the library learning how to find *a better job*. Ask the librarian to point you to books on career development and job search strategies. Look at sample resumes and cover letters but don't stop there, read success stories and job search strategies that relate to your employment issues or desired career development. Look for sample resumes and cover letters that describe positions similar to the ones that you've held and consider using language from those samples to revitalize your own employment documents.

If your work history is blemished by a period of unemployment or an involuntary termination, look for strategies that will help you address those issues. If you have a prison record, go the extra mile and search the web for articles and special programs designed to help ex-offenders ...**then follow up!**

Finally, while you are at the library improving your employment documents and learning how to search for a job, spend some time on the Internet getting familiar with the major job sites like **Indeed.com**.   If you believe you need job skills, start by accessing the job market to find out what job skills are in demand for the type of job you would like. Then consider whether you can get those skills and improve your marketability through free or low cost online resources. Look for job training programs in your community or at your local community college. Remember the knowledge you need is everywhere and in many cases it is free. So, go after it! And understand, you will heighten your *faith to find a job,* if you know that you have first-rate employment documents and a winning strategy to find a good job.

> *"**A wise man will hear and increase learning,** and a man of understanding will attain wise counsel..."*
> *(Proverb 1:5)*

Reality Check: *An accepted definition of wisdom involves making the best use of knowledge. Knowing what to do, but not doing it is foolish.*

Chapter 9

The Beauty of the Lord... Job Interviews

"...let the beauty of the LORD our God be upon us, and establish the work of our hands for us..." (Psalm 90:13-17)

The store was closing but this particular customer was determined to shop up until the very last minute...until she had to leave. *I was trying to help her, but it wasn't easy.* She was extremely stressful and ill-mannered because she had an important job interview the next morning, but she did not have anything flattering to wear. She was overweight and looking for something that would slenderize her figure, but her funds were limited. Therefore, she was limited to the sales rack. Finally, the dreaded announcement came...the store was closing, and she had to leave *without* an interview outfit.

We can all agree, it's very important that you make a good impression when going on a job interview. In fact, it's best to plan what to wear before you get the call. Waiting until the last minute to put an interview outfit together will cause unnecessary stress just *before* the interview and may cause you to feel self-conscience about how you look *during* the interview. The right outfit on the other hand, can convey a positive first impression to a potential employer *and help you relax about your appearance.*

.   In truth, your clothes should give you a good visual introduction, but once you start talking, they should fade into the background so you and your qualifications can shine. If you're dressed shabbily or inappropriately, or if you're overdressed or too sexy your appearance will be center stage and may end up detracting from the interview.

In planning your outfit, dress for the job you're interviewing for but *use common sense.* I knew a very feminine young woman who was up for a good paying manual labor job who told me she wore work boots and jeans to her interview because she wanted to convey that she was up to the demands of manual labor. It was a risky strategy, but she said it worked. She was offered the job she believes, because she went to the interview looking like she could handle the work. Conversely, if you're up for a job where you would be working with the public and formal business attire is viewed as an asset, then by all means, wear your nicest clothes and dress the part. If you're trying to sell an employer on your creative qualifications, it's alright to reveal *a bit* of the artist inside ...but again, use common sense...and don't go to the extreme.

For the rest of us, I think a *high-end business casual* look is the best strategy. For men, that means you should wear, minimally, a dress shirt (preferably white), a tie and a nice pair of dress pants. Corduroy and khaki may be fine for the office *after* you get the job, but for the interview process, wear dress pants and a tie. If you're up for a management position, you should include a suit jacket or a nice business suit. If you're up for a position of authority or an executive position, you'll need a polished business suit.

Minimally, women should consider pairing a moderate blouse with a knee length skirt or a nice pair of dress pants. A conservative dress is also a good option, but avoid casual and sheer fabrics, prints and frilly overly feminine styles. If you're up for a management position, a business skirt suit or pant suit is an ideal choice. And if you're up for an executive position or a position of authority, again, you'll need to add more polish to your look.

In recent years, *business casual* has revolutionized most office dress codes. However, in adopting new dress codes, many companies have also adopted detailed policy about the type of dress that is *not* acceptable. So, for a job interview in a business office, its best to step the business casual look up a notch and choose a relatively conservative look. Moreover, keep in mind that you should never wear gym shoes, tee shirts, jeans, an ultra-short skirt, shorts, or body piercings to an interview. Women can wear a pair of pierced earrings, but that is not recommended for men. Finally, if possible cover any tattoos and style your hair and make-up appropriately for a business environment.

And **why should you be anxious about clothes?** *Consider the lilies of the field and learn thoroughly how they grow; they neither toil nor spin.*

But if God so clothes the grass of the field, which today is alive and green and tomorrow is tossed into the furnace, will He not much more surely clothe you, O you of little faith?

(Matthew 6: 28 and 30 - Amplified Bible)

If you're on a budget and can't afford interview clothes, don't panic. You can find beautiful high quality clothes at a fraction of their retail price at second hand stores and resale shops. That's where I found *all* my interview outfits. If you go this route, be mindful of the fact that you may not be able to try on your selections, so you'll have to *know your size and the styles that look best on you.* If you're not sure what size you wear in business clothes, or how to put a nice look together, then go to a retail store *first* and try on several outfits. *Remember you are not buying, so try on clothes that reflect the way you really want to look on a job interview.* Try on a several nice outfits and pay attention to size, fabric quality and the way the retailer displays various outfits in the store. Then, armed with your sizes and an image of how you want to look, head for the resale shop.

When shopping at second hand stores, look for classic styles and high quality fabrics. Don't buy anything faded or worn, even if you like the style. Black and navy blue are ideal for business dressing, but don't try to turn a pair of pants and a jacket of the same color into a suit if the fabrics and colors are not *perfectly identical.* It's better to contrast the color of the pants and a jacket if the fabric threading doesn't match. Women have more options to work with along these lines, but for men its best to choose a classic combination like gray pants, a white shirt, and either a navy blue or black blazer. Black, brown, or navy-blue dress pants can also be matched with a nice tweed jacket that complements the color of the pants.

At a good resale shop, twenty-five dollars (maybe less) will probably buy anybody a nice interview outfit, but then go the extra mile and have your purchase cleaned at a professional dry cleaner. If possible, try to acquire at least two appropriate outfits in case you're asked to come back for a second round of interviews.

Knowing that you're ready for a job interview will motivate you to work hard to get one. And when the time comes, knowing that you have the right clothes will help you relax about your appearance and elevate your faith that your appearance is working for, and not against you.

Tips to Help Your Job Interview Go Well

➢ *Exercise and eat right when you are job hunting.* Eating a diet that is rich in fruits and vegetables will help you look your best and manage the stress associated with your employment search and the interview process. Drink plenty of water daily and exercise at least four or five times a week. If you don't have a favorite workout routine try a walking program.

➢ *Embrace your best personal hygiene.* When going on a job interview it pays to be extra clean and to wear colognes and perfumes *lightly*, if at all.

➢ *Plan your makeup and hair style*. Women, your planning should include one *or two* trips to a cosmetic counter at a fine department store. Allow a make-up artist to do your face, but be sure to tell him or her that you want a natural look appropriate for a job interview. Generally, you don't have to pay anything for this service, and you may walk away with a few valuable samples. More importantly, if you like the outcome, note the colors that look good on your face and the way the makeup was applied. Then go out and purchase affordable cosmetics and practice making up your face at home. Get comfortable styling your hair and applying your makeup so you don't have to stress about those details on the day of your interview.

➢ ***Go to the interview prepared.*** Take a copy of your resume, the cover letter you sent the company, and your employment data sheet. If you don't have an application on file, many companies will ask you to fill one out just before the interview, so take your employment data sheet to eliminate the stress associated with completing the application properly.   Also, learn something about the company that you are interviewing with and prepare one or two questions about the company or the position. Lastly, find and read articles about interviewing techniques and strategies to explain gaps in your employment history or an involuntary termination.

➢ ***Complement your positive appearance with a totally positive attitude.*** Even if your job history includes a really rotten job, don't talk badly about your past employers or supervisors. If you left a job under negative circumstances, think of a positive professional way to frame your experience.   Be prepared to answer every question but don't volunteer negative information or insights. Indeed, in a job interview, the old adage is true; if you don't have anything positive to say...it's best to say nothing at all.

➢ ***Don't hard sell your qualifications or boast and brag about your accomplishes.***   Pride is repulsive but humility is attractive, so do your best to exude confidence and humility and use your accomplishments as a mean to demonstrate the effectiveness of your skill sets.

➢ *Send a thank you note after your interview*. Ask for a business card or write down the names of the individuals that you interview with, then after the interview follow up with an email of appreciation. Thank the interviewer(s) for their time and mention something that was said, to demonstrate that you were listening. Examples of these types of communications can be found in resume and cover letter books or online at career development sites.

"Be anxious for nothing, but in everything by prayer and supplication, with thanksgiving, let your requests be made known to God and the peace of God, which surpasses all understanding, will guard your hearts and minds through Christ Jesus". (Philippians 4: 6-7)

Finally, pray and ask God to provide you with the right clothes to wear, to anoint and enable you to do your best, and to grant you *favor* with those who will be evaluating your qualifications. Remember anxiety is a call to prayer, so pray until you sense God's peace. Do not structure your faith around your appearance or interview skills, but meditate on the truth of God's word, that through Christ, you can do all things. **Through Christ you can do really well in a job interview.**

Reality Check: If you had a job interview tomorrow, would you be prepared? If not, start preparing today! You'll eliminate a lot of pre-interview anxiety if you're not worried about how you'll look.

Faith to Find a Job

Chapter 10

Due Diligence

"But what do you think? A man had two sons, and he came to the first and said, 'Son, go, work today in my vineyard.' He answered and said, 'I will not,' but afterward he regretted it and went. Then he came to the second and said likewise. And he answered and said, 'I go, sir,' but he did not go.

Which of the two did the will of his father?"
They said to Him, "The first." Matthew 21:28-31

In Chapter 8 I shared that during my last job search, I worked as a substitute teacher and a retail sales associate for a large department store. During that time, the store was preparing for a visit by a world class dignitary and each department was asked to spruce up and help put the store in its best condition. The manager of the women's dress department where I worked responded to the call by cleaning out a storage room where we kept a rack of clothes that belonged in other departments. There were a couple hundred items that needed to be returned to various stations throughout the full length and breadth of three floors. The project would require a lot of heavy lifting and walking, so our manager asked several of us to share the burden of putting the clothes away.

*A false balance is **abomination** to the LORD: but a just **weight** is his delight. (Proverbs 11:1)*

It was a nasty job that nobody, including me, wanted to do but each of the seven or eight sales associates that were commissioned to get the job done, immediately responded by grabbing a handful of clothes and going off into various directions to put them away. All of us were supposed to pitch in and work until the entire rack of clothes had been returned; but after about three or four trips back to the rack, I realized that I was the only one still working at the project. *Everyone else* had gone back to their normal duties. Some of them were socializing and waiting around for customers, and some of them were probably laughing at me because I was still putting clothes away.

At that point, it would have been easy for me to quit and give up because everyone else had. I had done more than my *fair share*, and I could have complained to the department manager and excused myself for abandoning the project before it was completed. However, as I continued working and wrestling with the best way to handle the situation, I kept returning to my faith in God and a personal sense of integrity that would not allow me to walk away just because everyone else had ...and just because the work was hard. I had never willfully ignored a supervisor's directive, and I wasn't going to start that day just because my co-workers decided to. So I kept working for the next couple of hours *by myself* until all the clothes had been put away.

I have no idea if my supervisor was ever made aware of how the project was eventually accomplished, because I did not do it to impress her. I did it because I believed that the eyes of God were watching me, and I knew that it was God's expectation that I do the right thing. However, I also deeply believed that **God would reward my hard work and righteous choices.**

*For I say to you, that unless your **righteousness exceeds** the*

righteousness *of the scribes and Pharisees, you will by no means enter the kingdom of heaven. (Matthew 5:20)*

*"For **God is not unrighteous to forget your work and labor of love**, which ye have showed toward his name, in that ye have ministered to the saints, and do minister. And we desire that every one of you do show the same **diligence** to the full assurance of hope unto the end: That **ye be not slothful,** but followers of them who through faith and patience inherit the promises."*
(Hebrews 6:10-12 - King James Version)

One of the tenets that shaped my sense of integrity that day came out of my studies in the field of education. *Motivation* is an important topic to educators because they want to understand why some students are motivated to succeed while others are not. *Why do some students go on to achieve their academic goals while others don't?* The problem is complex and not always easy to understand, but I remember hearing an observation along these lines that I've often pondered and allowed to shape my approach to life. The observation is this: *Achievers work until the job is done. The requirements of accomplishing the task dictate the effort they put forth. Underachievers, on the other hand, only work when they feel like it! The effort they put forth is tied to how they feel about the work at hand ...and not the effort required to accomplish the task.* Achievers, so defined, tend to be self-motivated while underachievers, defined in this way, often need external pressure to motivate them to finish a task.

Jesus said to them, "My food is to do the will of Him who sent Me, and to finish His work. (John 4:34)

Faith to Find a Job

Laziness is all about how we feel about the work. My daughter is a highly accomplished college student and nurse, but when she was a little girl I noticed that she always had the energy to play, but when it was time to do her chores she would always tell me she was **tired**. Time and again, I watched her energy level diminish *in seconds*, when it was time to do her housework.

Job hunting is not always an easy task, it *may* require you to spend some time at the library reading books on conducting a successful job search. It *may* require you to write and re-write your resume and cover letters. It *may* require you to spend *regular time* on the Internet searching for a job. It *may* require you to learn an additional job skill. And the premise behind *Faith to Find a Job* is that it *will* also require you to pray and spend time reading, meditating and confessing the Word of God.

On the other hand, looking for a job *may* also require you to give up some things that you normally enjoy. To find time to conduct a successful job search, you *may* have to give up some of the time usually spent watching television. You *may* need to give up time you would like to spend hanging out with friends or talking on the phone. Money that you *might* like to use to buy a new pair of jeans and a tee shirt may need to be spent on a conservative interview outfit that doesn't really reflect your sense of style. A successful job search *may* take months of hard work and sacrifice, and you *may* need to persevere despite the results ...but that is where our faith comes in. If we do the hard work and sacrifice *under the eyes of God ...as unto the Lord,* then we can have confidence that God will reward our diligent effort.

Faith to Find a Job

*But without faith it is impossible to please him: for he that cometh to God must believe that he is, and that **He is a rewarder of them that diligently seek him.(Hebrews 11:6**)*

Look at Hebrew 11:6 and then understand that most people believe that *God is...*but only a small percentage of folks believe He will reward their diligent efforts. None of us need to think that faith in God's goodness is all we need to produce an abundant harvest, but hear me because I am saying that *all we need to produce an abundant harvest is* **faith in God's Word.**

You see if we really believe God's Word it will motivate us to *do* the right thing ...even when everyone around us is not. *God's rich promise* of an overflowing harvest *is dependent upon acting on His Word.* If we sow abundantly, we will reap abundantly. (2 Corinthians 9:6). If we persist, we'll get what we're after. (Luke 11:5-13). If we get wisdom, it will exalt us and bring us prosperity (Proverb 4:1-9). Indeed, if we honestly believe God's Word, we will *act on it* ...regardless of how it looks to everyone else.

*Who then is a **faithful and wise servant**, whom his lord hath made ruler over his household, to give them meat in due season? Blessed is that servant, **whom his lord when he cometh shall find so doing**. Verily I say unto you, That he shall make him ruler over all his goods. But if that evil servant shall say in his heart, My lord delayeth his coming; And shall begin to smite his fellow servants, and to eat and drink with the drunken; The lord of that servant shall come in a day when he looketh not for him, and in an hour that he is not aware of, And shall cut him asunder, and appoint him his portion with the hypocrites: there shall be weeping and gnashing of teeth. (Matthew 24:45-51)*

Faith to Find a Job

I don't know about you, but I find this particular passage of scripture humbling. I am not *always* a faithful and wise servant. Indeed, there have been times when I've lingered too long at a co-workers desk *just talking* when I should have been at my own desk *working.* And other times when I've taken a stroll on the Internet, when I know I should have been focused on the work that I am being paid to do. Sure some of this is just the relaxed customs of the office environment but in truth, if I don't watch myself. I will offend myself. It makes me uneasy when I fall short of the high standard of righteousness that I believe the Lord is calling us to live out. *God's eyes are always watching,* always calling us to faithfulness and integrity because He wants to bless us. God's righteousness *produces* His blessings, just as our wickedness produces a curse.

> *"He who covers his sins will not prosper, but whoever confesses and forsakes them will have mercy.*
>
> *Whoever walks blamelessly will be saved, but he who is perverse in his ways will suddenly fall.*
>
> *A faithful man will abound with blessings."*
>
> *(Proverbs 28:13, 18 and 20)*

Know, that even if you're believing for a position as the Chief Executive Officer of a Fortune 500 corporation, you will to some extent be signing on as a servant to the company. All of us, no matter what position we are believing for, must realize that God is calling us to serve with faithfulness, wisdom and integrity. God has promised to bless us and make us a blessing (Genesis 12:1-3). He wants to answer our prayer for a good job, but He also wants us, as employees, to be an answer to prayer. So live your life under the eyes of God. Do the job you are being paid to do with excellence as though you were working for the Lord. Confess and forsake your sins in this area and cultivate integrity as an employee. Be diligent about your job search and every task that you are responsible for doing.

Reality Check: *Looking for a job can be hard work but God can anoint you and give you a **holy ease** that will enable you to do all that needs to be done to succeed. (I Kings 18:46)*

Chapter 11

God Gives the Increase

"It is written, 'Man shall not live by bread alone, but by every word of God." (Luke 4:3-4)

All we need to produce an abundant harvest is **faith in God's Word.** That's the power point that I want you to remember from the last chapter. If the long list of things that you *may* need to do or give up, seems a bit daunting, remember...it *may not* take all that. In an earlier chapter I shared how I prayed, sent out some resumes and it all came together in one month. A few years down the line however, my job search required a lot more. I share both scenarios because, I want you to have a *comprehensive understanding* of the challenge of searching for a good job...even *by faith.* I want you to honestly evaluate how you feel about the work required to accomplish your goals. And I want you to understand, that how you feel about the work does not have to have the final say.

For me, it is helpful to know that the way I feel about work can zap my motivation and detour me from accomplishing a goal. Just understanding *that* has been enough to motivate me to fight back and push pass my own tendency to do less than the best. **Achievers** fight their own lazy spirits, they take stock of what needs to be done, and then they go out and do it! God's Word inspires us to go out and do it in a right way. And it encourages us to believe that if we do, the Lord of the Harvest will reward our diligent efforts.

"Now it shall come to pass, if you diligently obey the voice of the LORD your God, to observe carefully all His commandments

Faith to Find a Job

The LORD will command the blessing on *you in your storehouses and in* **all to which you set your hand,***"(Deuteronomy 28:1 and 8)*

Faith to Find a Job is a bible study that is jam packed with hope-filled scriptures that encourage you to believe that your effort will produce results. These scriptures do not encourage us to believe that our work is not necessary, but they encourage us to believe that the *Lord of the Harvest* will bring forth results. *He will bless all that you set your hand to; He will reward your diligent effort.*

Understand, the Bible was written during the *agricultural revolution.* In the first few pages of Genesis we see *the father of The Faith*, Abraham, looking for *land.* Before people learned to farm, they were hunters and gatherers moving from place to place in search of food. Hunters and gatherers lived in perpetual survival mode... hunger was always a threat. When people learned to farm however, they could settle on the land and their mastery of the environment enabled them to bring forth a massive provision of food. Back then however, people also had a fundamental understanding that skill was not enough to master the environment. No matter how skillfully and diligently they worked to farm the land, if the **Heavens** did not give forth **rain** ...there would be no harvest.

"Then the LORD appeared to him and said: "Do not go down to Egypt; live in the land of which I shall tell you. Dwell in this land, and I will be with you and bless you...

Then Isaac sowed in that land, and reaped in the same year a hundredfold; and the LORD blessed him. **The man began to prosper, and continued prospering until he became very**

prosperous; *for he had possessions of flocks and possessions of herds and a great number of servants. So, the Philistines envied him. (Genesis 26:2,3 and 12-14)"*

It would be such a mistake to invest *your faith* in hard work, in sending out resumes, networking and searching the Internet for a job. Searching for a job will *increase your faith* that you will find a job, but like Isaac, in the verse above, you need to understand fundamentally that **God gives the increase.** God is the Lord of the Harvest. Isaac got the blessing because he had a personal on-going relationship with God. Like his father Abraham, Isaac was a man of faith. In Genesis 24:63, we see Isaac going out into the fields in the evening to spend time with God...*to meditate.* Isaac was a man of prayer, *a friend of God* and that was the key to his prosperity...and that is the key to ours.

*"... and **as long as he sought the LORD, God made him** to prosper." (2 Chronicles 26:5)*

God created man for a divine relationship. He desires us to talk to Him during the good and bad times. God called Abraham *His friend* and Jesus called God, *Abba...which means Daddy!* Friendship and fatherhood are relationships that characterize the ways we should be relating to God. *Can you say that God is your friend? Your Daddy?* A friend would help you find a job. A Daddy would provide your needs. However, many of us don't have that type of relationship with God. We are so busy with life, social media, our friends, television and movies, with using drugs or other things that cloud our minds, that we don't have time or an interest in a relationship with God. Even so, we want God to give us the ongoing abundant prosperity He gave Isaac, but we do not want to give God what Isaac gave *...regular fellowship in God's presence.*

If the idea of spending time with God seems like a chore, then you don't understand what Abraham, Isaac and Jesus understood, that in God's presence is everything you will ever need ... exceedingly and abundantly above all that you can think or ask (Ephesians 3:20). Praying when you're in trouble or when you need or want something really badly is not a relationship with God, but it may explain why your prayers go unanswered. Even so, as important as prayer is, it is only a one-sided conversation. Real relationships are two-sided, they include conversations that involve talking *and listening.*

"Jesus answered and said unto them, **Ye do err, not knowing the scriptures,** *nor the power of God.*

*...***have ye not read that which was spoken unto you by God.***

(Matthew 22:29 and 31)

Jesus asked the question, Have you not **read** what was **spoken?** Have you not read what was **spoken by God?** God and His Voice and His Power are in the sacred scriptures (John 1:1). Reading the Bible is the other side of the relationship, the other side of our conversation with God. Getting quiet and reading God's word is how we hear from God. In fact, God has said *success, good success* is in His Word ...in reading it, speaking it, and meditating on it (Joshua 1:8).

Faith to Find a Job

This is a call to repentance. Don't *just* read the encouraging words in this book, pull out your Bible and look up the scripture citations at the end of the statements that encourage you. Write down the scriptures that mean something special to you and think about them *instead* of your fears. When I partnered with God in believing for a good job I didn't have a life coach to give me a comprehensive understanding of what it takes to search for a job by faith. All I had was prayer and my Bible. So I would be remiss if I lead you to believe that you need anything **less**. No matter how encouraging the words in this book may be ...there is nothing as inspiring and rock solid as God's Word *received in faith from God.*

Faith to Find a Job

Cultivating a Warmer Relationship with God

A warm relationship with God starts by devoting time to that relationship. It doesn't have to be hours a day or even an hour each day, but it should be a consistent daily routine of prayer and fellowship with the Lord and His Word. Following are a few suggestions to help you develop a warmer relationship with God.

Now in the morning, having risen a long while before daylight, He went out and departed to a solitary place; and there He prayed. (Mark 1:35)

➤ **Use a daily devotional.** Daily devotionals like *The Upper Room* or *Our Daily Bread* are wonderful tools for directing our thoughts towards God on a daily basis. Once you find a devotional you like, analyze your daily routine and look for 15 or 20 minutes that you're alert and can focus on reading the devotional and accompanying scripture citations. Then even if it's only 5 minutes a day *make time for prayer.* You can find daily devotionals online or if you prefer a booklet, you can order devotional booklets online.

*"Then Jesus said to His disciples, "If anyone desires to come after Me, let him deny himself, and take up his cross, and follow Me. For whoever desires to save his life will lose it, but **whoever loses his life for My sake will find it.**" (Matthew 16:24-25)*

➤ **Fast whatever is getting in the way.** Sometimes our flesh can stand in the way of developing a relationship with God. Our flesh does not want to pray or read the Bible ...it wants to eat all day, watch TV all night and spend all our extra money shopping online. Our flesh might be a workaholic, a pornography addict, or it may just want to talk on the phone and do *anything but* pray and read the Bible. Even so, the fact remains that if we want a more meaningful relationship with our Heavenly Father...if we want answered prayers and miracle provisions, then we will need to deny ourselves some of those selfish pleasures and sacrifice ourselves instead to God. In order to make *space in our minds* for the Lord we may need to go on a *media fast* or a *spending fast* and learn how to respect the Sabbath. We may even have to give up some relationships that are contrary to the direction that God is speaking into our lives. *Our problems are physical, so our fast must be physical.*

A regular routine of *fasting food* can help us connect to the right spiritual priorities. Consider for a period of time (21 days) giving up sweets and desserts and following the other specifications of the **Daniel Fast** (Daniel 10:2-3). Alternatively, you can start a spiritual fitness routine by Elijah fasting (going in the strength of the food). **Elijah fasting** *requires that* you eat a sensible meal, *give up snacking and lustful eating between meals,* and eat again only when you're hungry. To that routine, you can begin replacing one regular meal, once or twice a week, with coffee, tea, plain water or nothing at all.

In whatever way you feel lead, ease into a routine of fasting, knowing that God will honor your sacrifice with answered prayer and the miracle provisions promised in His word.

Faith to Find a Job

Reality Check: *Fasting is a private act of faith between you and God that is connected to a marvelous promise. If you fast privately, Jesus said, God will bless you openly. (Matthew 6: 16-18)*

Chapter 12

Networking

*For whoever **exalts** himself will be **humbled**, and he who **humbles** himself will be **exalt**ed." (Luke 14:11)*

One Sunday after church about twelve of us were packed into a church van heading to a commuter train, when I heard a voice behind me from the back of the van holler out, *"Hey everybody! I am a college student and I am looking for a summer job ...maybe a paid internship. If anyone has a lead or knows of a company hiring for the summer, I would really appreciate your help."*

I did not say anything but right away I was convicted because my company had a paid internship program for college students ...so I considered that maybe God wanted me to help this young man. We go to the same church, and I had seen him on several occasions before that afternoon, *but* I still didn't feel comfortable giving out my personal contact information. So as we road along, I quietly wrote my name and business email address on a slip of paper, and when I got off the van I waited for him. When we connected, I gave him my email address and told him to send me his resume. I explained that I worked for a company in the Chicago Loop that sponsored a paid summer internship for college students, and if he sent me his resume, I promised I would forward it to our recruiting director.

The next morning when I logged on to my workstation, there in my inbox was an email from this young man with a copy of his resume attached. His email expressed a mature appreciation for my help that made me feel good about getting involved ...but when I opened the attachment and read his resume, I could see that it was clearly in no shape to forward to my HR Department. I mean, his resume was poorly written and organized, and it didn't reflect well on him *or me!* When I read it, I realized my divine mission was to do more than just receive and pass on his resume. I felt the Lord wanted me to help this young man improve his resume.

Now understand, sometimes I think I have an invisible flashing neon sign on my forehead that reads: "Need Help with Your Resume ...Ask Me!" Over the years I have helped so many people; family, friends ...and complete strangers write or improve their resumes that I have come to believe it is part of my **divine call.**

It all started right after college, my degree is in Applied Industrial Psychology, which is a type of HR degree. In an academic setting at the University of Illinois, I learned how to develop various types of employment documents such as job descriptions and procedures. The basic unit of most of these employment documents is the *task description*. It was many years ago, but I can still see the look on my professor's face when I finally got the hang of writing task descriptions.

In any case, the basic unit of a resume is also *a type of task description,* ergo when someone would ask me to look at their resume, because of my academic background, I would generally have a lot to say. In fact, I would usually end up reorganizing and rewriting portions of the document. So then the word got out in the family and among our friends, if you need help with your resume to **ask me.** Anyway, that's how this ministry was born.

It's never been a burden because I have a passion for helping people in this way. Sometimes I can't resist myself. Like that Monday morning when I looked at that young man's resume, I didn't hesitate. I had plenty to do at work and at home...really, I didn't need another project, but somehow I knew I would make time to help this young man revise his resume.

*... doing the will of God from the heart, with goodwill doing service... knowing that **whatever good anyone does, he will receive the same from the Lord...**" (Ephesians 6:6-8)*

Over the next week or so, I exchanged dozens of emails with the young man as we worked to revise his resume. I questioned him about his academic achievements, summer jobs, volunteer experience, church involvement, computer aptitude and specials skills. And I found out that he was quite accomplished. This young man had office experience, good computer skills and typed 70 wpm. When I finished his resume, I passed it on to the recruiting director at my company, but I also suggested that he look into a temporary employment agency. He was always dressed so polished and neat at church, and he had an air of sophistication that seemed ideal for an office environment.

In any case, apparently I wasn't the first person to suggest that he try a temporary employment agency as a way to find summer work. A year earlier his aunt made the same suggestion but when he followed through, it turned out disastrously. He said, he did really well on the skills tests but when the employment counselor asked him what type of salary he was looking for, and he told her...*she laughed in his face.* He said he felt so humiliated and embarrassed that he vowed *never* to trust an employment agency again.

> *And they ridiculed Him. But... He... put them all outside.*
> *(Mark 5:40)*

Let us stop here and begin to evaluate some of the things this young man did right and some of the things that I think were *serious mistakes.*

First, he did two things that were really well; he used a network strategy to look for a job, and he followed up on a job lead in an extremely professional way.

The two mistakes he made were; he *sent out a resume that did not make him look attractive as a job candidate,* and *he allowed rejection to influence his job search.*

These issues are all important to the process of searching for a job as well as building our faith to find a job. So in the next Chapter, we will go into a more detailed discussion on developing a *first rate resume,* and in a later chapter, we will explore a strategy for standing against rejection and building faith that God will give us divine favor in the selection process. For the rest of this chapter, however, we will look at the main thing this young man did right. **He used a bold networking strategy to look for a job.**

I applaud this young man for using a **networking strategy** to search for a job. Networking is probably the most overlooked strategy for finding a job because the majority of us want to be viewed as being self-sufficient. Most people don't want to need anyone or ask anyone for help. On top of that, unemployment or underemployment and the related financial strain, often leave some feeling embarrassed and ashamed about their economic situation. Even so, we still need to humble ourselves and *spread the news* that we're looking for a job ...because **a recommendation from a well-respected person** *who is already on staff at an organization* **can have a profound impact on a hiring decision.**

People who are working can provide us with job leads, and **if they are willing and able** they can also provide us with a recommendation that could help us get a job ...and in some cases help them get a referral bonus. Nevertheless, **only people who think they know you** will be able to recommend you for a position.

I know a woman who recently landed a pretty good job this way. She was convinced that the only way she was going to get on at a good company was if someone of influence gave her a recommendation. So she kept asking around until her sister, who had a very high level position at an organization, recommended her for an administrative job at a different office. The woman got the job and in less than a year she was up for a promotional opportunity based solely on her own merits. This story has a happy ending, but it doesn't always turn out that way. In fact, some of the people that know you and love you may be reluctant to recommend you for a position at their company *because they are not acquainted with your work ethic.*

Faith to Find a Job

Your acquaintances may know you as their carefree friend who loves to party every weekend or their cool cousin with the incredibly sloppy bedroom. Your image may be socially acceptable but your acquaintances may honestly, have doubts about you as an employee. They may even fear that if you get a job at their company, and it doesn't work out, that your negative performance might end up reflecting badly on their professional reputation. Moreover, they may fear that if you both work for the same company, your expectation would also include an expanded social connection that they may not really desire.

Do not take your family and personal acquaintances for granted but approach these individuals with the same respect you would give someone you did not know as well. Inform people you know that you are looking for a job and ask them to provide you with any job leads they may hear about. Don't pressure a family member or friend to give you a recommendation at their place of employment. However, if you think they may be reluctant to help you because they are not familiar with your work ethic, then respectfully give them a run down on your career accomplishments and qualifications. If you think it will help, provide them with a copy of your resume and talk about your professional ethics or anything else that may be of concern. Then from time to time, respectfully follow up to see if the hiring climate at their organization has changed.

"...make friends for yourselves by unrighteous mammon, that when you fail, they may receive you into an everlasting home..."(Luke 16:9)

Hollering out in a church van may seem a bit over the top, but it was highly effective and not out of place for that group of *familiar faces* who share a house of worship each Sunday. Still, announcing to a group of *complete strangers* that you are looking for a job is generally not a good idea. You'll probably end up looking like a flake and instead of a job lead you'll be the recipient of a few really strange stares. However, if you have an opportunity to develop a conversation with a person at a bus stop, in line at the grocery store, or as you're waiting at the barber shop, then it's perfectly appropriate to mention that you are looking for a job. I even think it's fitting to ask that person if their company is hiring and if so, ask for the contact information so you can **independently** initiate an application. If the person *offers* to pass on your resume, ask for their business contact information, perhaps a business email address and **then follow up.**

Finally, understand that **job fairs** are really networking events. However, if you've ever attended one, then you'll know they can be overwhelming in terms of the number of people who are trying to get to and impress the recruiters. Recently, I heard a woman tell how she waited patiently at a job fair to make a connection with a Fortune 500 company that she really wanted to work for. She said the company's booth was packed with interested job seekers, but she stuck it out and slowly inched her way up to the table. Once there, one of the recruiters mentioned that she had noticed her waiting a long time in the crowd, and that she admired her determination. Guest what? That encounter led to a job at that company.

Don't overlook job fairs but then don't overly try to impress recruiters once you're there. *Just go,* dress and act professionally. Pray and *trust God for* **favor** *with man*, because human encounters can be so unpredictable.

God...that's the only way I can explain how I got a job through a job fair. I walked up and introduced myself to a recruiter, and it turned out that we both had the same uncommon first name. That endeared her to me and prompted her to take a closer look at my resume. Then right there on the spot she gave me the contact information for her Regional Director. I followed up and within a week I had accepted a position. I didn't see that encounter as luck or strategy, but I considered it to be the providence of God. I was out seeking a job and true to the Lord's word, I found one.

"And God is able to make all **grace** *(every favor and earthly blessing) come to you in abundance, so that you may always and under all circumstances and whatever the need be* **self-sufficient** *[possessing enough to require no aid or support and furnished in abundance for every good work and charitable donation."*
(2 Corinthians 9:8 - Amplified Bible)

All of us want to be self-sufficient, and that is what God wants as well. However, God's plan for our provision often includes other people ...all grace, *favor* and earthly blessings abounding toward us through people He sends to help. So don't let your pride, shame or timidity get in the way. Get out and let people know you're looking for a job. Network, go to job fairs, hit the pavement, let family and friends know that you are looking. Seek, and you will find! Knock, and the door will be opened.

Chapter 13

A First-Rate Resume

"Cursed is the man who trusts in man
And makes flesh his strength....
Blessed is the man who trusts in the LORD,
And whose hope is the LORD." (Jeremiah 17: 5 and 7)

In the last chapter, we examined an encounter I had with a young college student that was looking for a summer job. I applauded his bold networking strategy, which brought him in contact with me and, which eventually produced a harvest of *a better resume.* Nevertheless, it didn't produce a harvest of a summer internship at my company. Of course there's no way of knowing for sure, but I wondered if he might have gotten an internship if his application had been a bit more timely. That leads me to what I believe is a cornerstone principle to an effective job search: **Don't start your job search with less than a first rate resume.**

To illustrate how strongly I feel about this principle, let's put some of what you know about me in perspective. I mentioned that I have an HR degree, that I have helped numerous people write and improve their resumes, and that I have conducted several successful job searches myself, yet in spite of all that, I also mentioned that I start every job search with **prayer.**

I start my job search by praying the *Prayer for Work* that is at the beginning of this book, Psalm 90:13-17. I ask God to *bless me* with a job, to establish the work of my hands *for me,* and to give me the resume and cover letter I need to get the job

He has for me. When I'm finished praying, ***I go to the library*** to look through career development books. I start the practical aspects of my job search at the library, because I know I need a first rate resume to get a first rate job. I also know that the best way to develop an effective resume is to spend time looking at and analyzing other effective resumes.

*"Trust in the LORD with all your heart And **lean not on your own understanding;** In all your ways acknowledge Him, And He shall direct your paths. **Do not be wise in your own eyes**; Fear the LORD and depart from evil..."(Proverbs 3: 5-8)*

As I began working with the young man from my church, I discovered that he was an excellent student. I also formulated the opinion that he could have done a much better job on his resume. The resume he initially sent didn't make him look good as a job candidate *nor did it reflect well on me as someone who was willing to give him a marginal endorsement.*

I've worked with several of our summer interns over the years. They were all full-time college students with very little work history. The resumes that I've seen (that made it through the selection process) highlighted academic and extracurricular accomplishments, skills and past work experience. They had an *excellent quality* because they were visually appealing, well-organized, and uniform in appearance.   The resume that I received from my young friend from church *did not have the same excellent qualities.* If fact, the style was inconsistent and overall it appeared to be disorganized.

*" A **good name** is to be chosen rather than great riches, loving favor rather than silver and gold." (Proverbs 22:1)*

Faith to Find a Job

Know that it is pointless to job search with a resume that doesn't make you look attractive as a job candidate. Writing resume content isn't rocket science nor is it all you need to know in order to develop a *first rate resume*. Nevertheless, *you can do it!* You can construct a resume with excellent qualities that makes it through the selection process, and everything you need is at your local library or on the Internet *for free*. Additionally, in this chapter we'll cover the basics of resume writing and provide you with a *Standard Resume Format* that you can use to structure a high quality resume. Even if you think you already have a first rate resume, and you're beyond the basic, reviewing these concepts might make it even better.

Four Essential Qualities of a First Rate Resume

Before you begin work on your resume, pray and ask God to give you the employment documents you need to get the job He has for you. Then remind yourself that the time you spend developing these vital documents is an investment in your future. Get in faith before you start working on your resume. Keep in mind, that your goal should always be to develop a first rate resume that has all the following qualities:

A ***first rate resume*** should be
1. *error free*
2. *visually appealing*
3. *organized and uniform*
4. composed of *well-written content*

1. ***Your Resume Should Be Error Free*** - The job market is highly competitive and your resume is your initial opportunity to convince a prospective employer that you are the best candidate for a job. The document itself introduces *you* and your potential work product. If your resume is unorganized, or if it contains spelling and grammatical errors, then a prospective employer might assume that it reflects the type of work you're likely to produce for their company. However, if your resume is polished, well organized and ***error free***, a potential employer may conclude that you are able to produce the same quality of work as an employee.

    When job hunting online, remember that many employers will request your resume in an electronic format. As I stated earlier, *word processing programs highlight spelling and grammatical errors*, so before you submit your resume in a word processing format, do a spelling and grammar check and resolve all related issues. Have someone with good communication skills proof read your documents and then, if possible submit your resume and cover letter in PDF format.

2. ***Your Resume Should Be Visually Appealing.*** A resume that is visually appealing creates a *good first impression* and helps your application stand out. Start the process by looking through resume and cover letter books and then choose a style that appeals to you and that looks attractive in both a hardcopy and electronic format. Analyze the style you like by looking for patterns in the way fonts are use and the way text is bolded, italicized or

underlined. Use fonts in the same manner as the style you choose. However, if you decide to vary the design, be careful to choose standard business fonts because the recipient of your documents may not have the ability to display a fancier font.

Your name should always appear at the top of your resume, though it doesn't matter if it is placed flush right, flush left or in the center. Contact information can be placed on your page in a variety of stylish ways but be sure to include your address and a least one telephone number where you can be reached. If you decide to include more than one telephone number, specify if it is your home, cell, or a work number. Finally, it is very common these days to see email addresses included with contact information. It is also equally common for a potential employer to attempt to contact you via an email address. So if you decide to include an email address use a *personal* account that you intend to *check frequently.*

3. ***Your Resume Should Be Organized and Uniform.*** *A lack of a consistent format is the most glaring mistake that people make when developing a resume, but one of the easiest problems to fix.* An example of an inconsistent format would be bolding a company name and underlining the job title for one position description, but in another description on the same resume, the company name appears in all capital letters and the job title is italics.

Study the **Standard Resume Format** on the next page and notice how various *print types are used consistently* to give the document an organized and uniform appearance. Notice first, that the *four major sections* (experience, skills, education and references) are distinguished by *capital letters.* Then notice that the EXPERIENCE section is further *organized* and presented in a *uniform manner.* The **Company Name**, **City and State** are always bolded and *Job Titles* are always presented underlined and in italics. Every company name and job title is presented on the resume in exactly the same manner. If for example, you started at a company as a *Retail Sales Associate,* and later you were promoted to *Assistant Store Manager,* list both titles under the **Company Name, City and State** with the most recent job title first. Moreover, use the job title your organization used to describe your job. Even if your supervisor referred to you as a *stock clerk* and that is how you thought of yourself, if your formal job title was *Inventory and Merchandise Specialist* than that is the title you should use on your resume.

Standard Resume Format

Your Name
Contact Information

EXPERIENCE
> **Company Name, City and State**
> *Job Title (Date)*
> Description of Responsibilities
> *Accomplishments*

> **Company Name, City and State**
> *Job Title (Date)*
> Description of Responsibilities
> *Accomplishments*

SKILLS (Optional)

EDUCATION
> **School Name, City and State**
> *Credential Detail (i.e. B.A. Political Science)*

REFERENCES
> *References will be provided upon request.*

Figure 13.1.

Standard Resume Format – Analysis

Ideally, your resume should be a highly organized one page document, that includes your name and contact information and details related to your work experience and formal education.

NAME AND CONTACT INFORMATION
Your name should always be highly distinctive and at the top of your resume. The rest of your contact information can be placed on your resume in a variety of stylish ways.

EXPERIENCE
Experience is usually the first major section of a resume. However, if your strongest credential is Education, then it should come before the Experience section. For instance, if you just finished a college degree or a specialized training program, but you don't have any career experience, place the Education section before Experience.

SKILLS and Other Optional Sections
Skills can often be developed independent of formal education and experience, and in many cases may turn out to be your strongest credential. If your typing speed is above average, or you can code in the newest programming language, highlight those skills on your resume. Other optional sections commonly found on resumes are CAREER OBJECTIVE or CAREER SUMMARY. These are brief narratives that are usually placed at the top of a resume that summarize your career interest or the breadth of your experience in a way that enhances your marketability.

EDUCATION
The Education section is usually found toward the bottom of most resumes and generally contains details about your formal high school or college credentials. However, you can enhance this section with specifics related to recent course work or certifications programs that you've completed.

REFERENCE
This is usually the last section of a resume and all that is required is a statement indicating that *references will be provided upon request.*

4. ***Your Resume Should Be Composed of Well Written Content -*** The EXPERIENCE section is usually the most detailed section of any resume, and it is also the *only* section that is *composed of written content* in contrast to factual details. More than any other aspect of developing a resume, describing job responsibilities is for many of us, the intimidating part of the process. If that expresses how you feel, then you definitely need to spend time exploring sample resumes and cover letters on the Internet and in career development books. Many of these resources explain in detail how to write resume content and many are organized by *job types*, so you can find actual job descriptions that you can use in your own resume.

To get you started however, in the next section we'll give you a **simple four step process** that will help you develop well-written descriptions of your job responsibilities. Keep in mind that *these descriptions should be written in **sentence case** and should contain action words that describe your **overall job responsibilities** but not necessarily each task.* For instance, your job responsibility may have included the tasks of *sweeping* and *mopping* the floor at the store where you worked. However, instead of trying to describe every task involved in keeping the store clean, **describe your overall responsibility,** which is to *"maintain a clean and orderly store environment."*

Faith to Find a Job

Four Steps to Writing Job Responsibility Descriptions

Step One: *On a separate sheet of paper, list all the job titles that you intend to include on your resume.* If your work history is extensive consider including only the most recent relevant ten years of experience. If you are considering changing careers, then you may want to include experience you gained outside of that time period. If that is the case, you may need to explore strategies related to the use of dates.

Step Two: *For each job title, describe your overall job responsibilities.* Again, do not try to write down everything you did or do. For instance, as a volunteer at your church you may *type correspondence for the ministerial staff and update and file giving records.* However instead of describing each task you may want to describe your overall responsibility which in this case might be to *provide administrative support to the ministerial staff.* Also, understand that you do not have to describe every aspect of a position. In fact, you can highlight certain aspects of a position and leave out others, depending on your search objectives. For instance, if you're currently working as an Administrative Assistant and one of your responsibilities include planning meetings and other office events. If you would like to steer your career in the direction of *events planning*, you may decide to go into more detail about your responsibility in this area and list accomplishments related to successful events that you've planned within prescribed budgets.

Finally, start every description on your list with an *action word* that describes how you carried out your responsibility. On the next page notice the action words used in *Example 1: maintaining, unloading, organizing, tracking* and *re-ordering. In Example 2*, the same description is presented in a bullet point format. In that format, the action words are in a different grammatical form: *unloaded, tracked,* and *re-ordered. Present tense* action words should be used to describe current positions and *past tense* action words to describe job responsibilities handled in the past.

Two Simple Formats: Describing Job Responsibilities

> ➤ **Example 1 (compound sentence style -** *conserves space***)**
> *Inventory and Merchandise Specialist:*

Responsible for maintaining a clean and orderly store environment, unloading shipments, and organizing inventory, tracking inventory levels and re-ordering merchandise as needed, stocking shelves, and developing special merchandise displays that appeal to customers.

Accomplishments: Routinely received commendations from Regional Manager regarding the cleanliness of the exterior and interior of the store.   Regularly selected to develop new merchandise displays at the front of the store. Promoted to Retail Sales Associate after only three months.

Figure 13..3

> ➤ **Example 2 (bullet point style -** *easy to write and read***)**
> *Inventory and Merchandise Specialist:*

- Worked to maintain a clean and orderly store environment,
- Unloaded shipments and organized inventory,
- Stocked shelves and developed special merchandise display that appealed to customers,
- Tracked inventory levels and re-ordered stock as needed.

Accomplishments: Routinely received commendations from Regional Manager regarding the cleanliness of the exterior and interior of the store.   Regularly selected to develop new merchandise displays at the front of the store. Promoted to Retail Sales Associate after only three months.

Figure 13.4

> ➤ **Step Three:**   *Transfer the list of job titles and responsibilities on to your resume.* Some employment counselors believe that *the bullet point style* used in

Example 2 is the most effective way to present a list of responsibilities on resumes and cover letters. The plus about using bullet points, is that it is easier to write and read. If your resume is incredibly detailed, on the other hand, you may want to maximize space by using the *compound sentence format* in *Example 1*. It's a good idea to *keep your resume to a one-page document* which means, you may only want to list your most central responsibilities and use a compound sentence style for *all* your descriptions. The most important thing to remember about Step Three is to use a consistent format throughout your resume. Also, if you decide to use the compound sentence format, be sure to *utilize commas and semi-colons appropriately.*

➤ **Step Four: *Analyze and proofread your resume.*** Make sure the facts and details included in your resume are accurate and verifiable. For instance, if a company has moved its office since you were employed there, use the most current location on your resume and not the location where you worked. Additionally, analyze your style and format choices and make sure you used consistent patterns to organize your resume. Finally, proofread your resume for spelling and grammatical errors and ask someone with good communications skills to proofread it.

➤

"I can do all things through Christ who strengthens me."
(Philippians 4:13)

Okay, you've got the basics now. With prayer and faith...*and knowledge...you can do it!* You can develop a first rate resume with excellent qualities that makes you look attractive as a potential employee. And with that in hand, you are ready to begin your search for a good job.

Chapter 14

Marketability... God's Plan

"Tell me, what do you have in the house? And she said,
Your maidservant has nothing *in the house* **but** *a jar of oil."*
Go, sell the oil and pay your debt, and you and your sons live on the rest." *(2King 4:2 and 7)*

It is a great feeling to earn a salary that more than covers all your living expenses, that allows you to save and enjoy a bit of life. That is the base line of what we're talking about when we're talking about finding a good job. If you have career experience or some sort of specialized training, then your job search probably has focus, and you have an idea of where to look, and what it will take to get that good job. However, if you're new to the job market, or if you believe you don't have any valuable job skills then you need to address the issue of your **marketability**, if you want to connect to that base-line good job that we just described.

So what do you have to offer an employer in exchange for that good job? That's the crux of marketability. Even so, the answer to that question does not start with a self-assessment or a college education... it starts with *an assessment of the job market.* What are employers looking for? Answer that question and you may discover that you have something valuable to offer? In fact, a careful assessment of the job market will not only help you find a good job in spite of a perceived lack of credentials, but it may also help you make a quality investment in career training.

Faith to Find a Job

"For which of you, intending to build a tower, does not sit down first and count the cost, whether he has enough to finish it." (Luke 14:28)

As I was approaching my last year of college, I decided to pick up some extra courses to qualify for a HR concentration in *Applied Industrial Psychology*, as opposed to, a general Psychology degree. I made that decision partly to increase my chances of finding a good job after graduation. Then a few months before I graduated, I started looking at *want ads* to find out what I needed in order to qualify for an entry-level HR position.

My degree was definitely a plus, but many of the advertised entry level positions indicated that a college degree was *optional.* In fact, what employers seemed to want most was *experience.* Still many employers were willing to train someone without experience or a degree if they had good typing and office skills. For the type of job I was looking for, it seemed like typing and office skills were more in demand than an advanced knowledge of HR management. So I knew what I had to do. I purchased a typing skills book, and I started spending almost every moment of my spare time doing drills to increase my accuracy and speed. After graduation, I even considered a self-study of shorthand and dictation, but before I had a chance to expand my skills training in that area, *a month after graduation,* I accepted a position as a *Personnel Secretary.*

In securing that position, I'm convinced that the results of my typing test helped me as much as my newly acquired college degree. But understand ...I did not have a typing certificate or a degree in office organization. In order to market my skills in this area, I had to prove that I could type *at an acceptable level.* I had taken typing in high school but in order to market that skill, I had to practice *and practice* until I reached a standard that an employer considered to be valuable. *I motivated myself* to improve my typing skills, but I also reviewed lessons related to structuring letters, envelopes and other business documents. Skills that I would need to succeed at an office job.

> *"Tell me, what do you have....? And she said,* **your maidservant has nothing ...but...."**

When I read the story of the desperate widow, I am always struck by the fact that the widow told the Prophet she had *nothing ...but.* It is as though she thought she had nothing of value ...but then remembered that she did indeed have a little something. That little something of value ...that after thought, is what God multiplied into a provision that more than met her needs.

Those of you who think you do not have any marketable job skills ...*think again.* Can you type? Can you drive? Are you good with people? Even if the only job you have ever had was working as a sales associate in a retail store or a fast food restaurant, then understand you have cash handling and basic accounting skills. In fact, you may have the basic skills you need to qualify for an entry-level position as a teller at a bank. The teller position might offer a slightly better salary, more stable hours, medical benefits, tuition reimbursement *and broader opportunities for advancement.* In assessing the job market you might start by exploring *company websites* associated with the financial industry. In doing so, you might be surprised to discover that your retail sales experience qualifies you for a variety of entry level positions. In fact, you might also discover that there are a good deal of jobs listed on those websites with nothing more than very general requirements like *high school diploma, good math and communication skills* or *customer service experience.*

Again, you'll need to assess the job market before you come to the conclusion that you don't have any marketable skills. To get an idea of what employers are looking for, explore company websites and on-line job banks like *Indeed.com.* When exploring on-line job banks you'll need some idea about the type of job you might want or think you're qualified for. If you're not sure where to get started then, use general terms like "Receptionist" "Driver" or "Administrative Assistant."

Redefining Yourself After a Layoff

Being laid off after a long successful career can be especially tough if you were employed in a highly specialized position or if your job was phased out in conjunction with advances in the industry. If that's the case, you may need to *redefine* yourself if you want to connect to another satisfying career position. Do you have excellent communication skills? Can you negotiate a contract? Are you an effective project manager or a top salesman? Think about marketing your *proven job skills* over and above your industry experience. Do the research and look for resume and cover letter strategies related to recovering your career or starting over after a job lay-off. Assess the job market and then stretch yourself and apply for jobs you believe you can do well, even if you do not have direct experience.

Faith to Find a Job

*Seeing at a distance a fig tree in leaf, He went to see if He would find anything on it. But **He found nothing**... Mark 11:13*

A Quality Investment in Career Training ... God's Plan

If you have accessed the job market and concluded that you need to pursue career training in order to find a really good job. Then know that you have come to one of the most important crossroads in your life. If ever there were a time to seek divine guidance, deciding on a career is that time. Acquiring job skills takes focus, discipline, and a commitment to learn all you can about the career that you hope to pursue. So, before you make what could be a life altering decision, start your journey with prayer. Specifically, ask the Lord to help you find *His plan for your life.*

Jeremiah 29:11 says the Lord has a good plan for your life. It is a plan to bless you, and not to harm you. Connecting to God's plan is the best thing that can ever happen to your life. So do not explore career paths and educational opportunities until you have prayed and asked for divine guidance.

Opportunity Abounds for Everyone

After you have prayed about it, if you decide to pursue a college credential and you have the time and money to pursue the opportunity *...that is fantastic.* However, if pursuing a college credential is out of the question because you need a more immediate solution or you don't have the money, have no fear, you can still find great job training opportunities that fit your lifestyle and budget.

Faith to Find a Job

These days there are so many free and inexpensive ways to gain marketable job skills, that just about anyone with a cellphone and access to the internet can pursue the knowledge they need to start a new or better career. Between YouTube and low-cost educational sites like Lynda.com, Udemy, and Coursera, opportunities abound for everyone. But understand, it takes a lot of confidence to market a job skill that is not evidenced by experience or a credential. Yet it is happening everyday by people who read job postings and believe they have the know how to do a job. When you believe you can do a job, your resume will take shape and you will be able to sell your skills and your knowledge base. But to get to that level of confidence, you will need to put in the time to educate yourself not just to get the job... but to do the job well once you get it.

I shared earlier in this chapter how I motivated myself to do a self-study of the office skills I believed would help me land the type of job I wanted. I studied and practiced until I developed the confidence to start applying for those types of positions. And I kept sharpening my skills until I got a job offer. Honestly, I do not believe I was successful in this endeavor because I am more disciplined than most people. I believe I prevailed because I was motivated to get a good job. I was willing to suspend my regular leisure activities to put the time and effort in to get the type of job I wanted. And if I can do it, you can do it too. You can do all things through Christ who strengthens you.

The power of the Lord came to Elijah. Then he ran ahead of King Ahab all the way to Jezreel. I Kings 18:46

Chapter 15

The Realities of the Job Market

*"Let your eyes look straight ahead, and your eyelids look right before you. **Ponder the path of your feet**, and let your ways be established." (Proverbs 4:26-27)*

In contemplating the topics to cover in this book, I knew that I had to talk about my pursuit of marketable skills apart from any benefit of having or not having a college degree. Too many young people these days, think that a college degree is a sure path to a good job and career success when that simply is not the case. For certain in-demand fields like nursing, teaching, information technology or engineering that assumption may be *relatively* true...but for other academic disciplines, particularly many liberal arts disciplines, a college degree will not necessarily ensure career success.

Not long ago I was talking to a neighbor, a really smart young lady who was preparing to head off to a four-year college. So, I asked if she had decided on a major. She told me that her favorite subject was History. She loved History but she also wanted to be a lawyer. Therefore, she said, she was planning to major in History and then go to law school. Her parents (and I agreed) thought that maybe she should consider majoring in History Education, so she could work as a teacher enroute to becoming a lawyer. This young lady, however, wasn't interested in becoming a teacher. She wanted to go straight to law school after college. So I told her about a conversation that I had with a young man about a year prior. He was a white male, he had just graduated from a first-rate law school, and he also had a

MBA from a top school. Nevertheless, he confided in me quite woefully, that neither he nor any of his friends from law school, had a decent job or a prospect for one. *"And in a few months,"* he told me with a lump in his throat, *"we have to start repaying our student loans."*

I did not want to discourage this young lady, but I wanted her to think soberly about what her value would be to the job market at the end of her educational journey. I told her that I had worked in the legal field for many years, and then I went on to share what I knew about the current job market for attorneys, which I discovered a few days later matched nearly word-for-word what the *Department of Labor* had published on the subject.

In truth, I'm more impressed with the employment options of a young man who I heard just finished his Associate degree in automotive mechanics, then I am about the future hopes of a college student who has not realistically pondered the benefits of a liberal arts degree and attending law school.

"The steps of a good man are ordered by the Lord, though he may stumble he will not utterly fall. Psalm 37:23

The young man who just finished training as an auto mechanic has a good full-time position already. While attending an affordable junior college, he was also working to support his wife and kids. Now in his mid-twenties he has career choices, marketable skills and a salary history that will positively impact his next job offer. As teenage parents, this young man and his wife (who is studying to be a teacher at a local community college) were forced to face *the realities of the job market.* As a young married couple with children, they are taking advantage of financial aid programs that not only cover college tuition but also, add a small income boost to those who qualify. This young couple may be struggling to raise their kids and make ends meet, but it sounds like they're making sound decisions about their future. And what's really *smart* about the way they're pursuing their careers...is that they found a debt free way to finance their college education.

> *"...the path of the just is like the shining sun, that shines ever brighter unto the perfect day. The way of the wicked is like darkness, they do not know what makes them stumble."*
> *(Proverbs 4:18-19)*

Listen before you invest big money in a college degree or a job training program...ponder the path of your feet. Visit the *Department of Labor* website and find out what you can about your career choice.

I don't want to discourage anyone from pursuing their interest or dreams, but I do want to encourage everyone to think *realistically* about the job market and their options for financing a college education or job training. So much is being publicized these days about people who are coming out of college with massive debt, but not much employment marketability. The *experience of going away to college* has for many parents and students, clouded the focus of what a college education is supposed to be about.

Years ago I decided to go to college because I wanted to increase my future earning potential. Like so many of my friends, I wanted to go away to college but *my wise mother did not see the benefit in taking out student loans to pay for me to live on campus, when I could get a perfectly good college education and live at home.* Furthermore, my older sisters and brother, now a teacher and administrator, a nurse and an administrator, and an attorney and judge, all started their college careers at local community colleges. My brother earned a B.S. in Chemistry and then worked full-time as an environmental chemist while he attended law school part-time. He and his wife paid his law school tuition themselves, so that when he finished his JD, he owed very little *if anything at all.* He's had an outstanding career as a State's Attorney in Illinois, and now he is a criminal court judge. And again, he started out at a local community college.

There is a way that seems right unto a man but in the end are the ways of death. Proverb 14:12

If you have a passion to become a lawyer, an actor, a musician, or anything else ...go for it, but do not ignore the realities of the job market. For instance, if you hope to be an artist, perhaps you should consider a minor in education or web design. Additionally, if you are contemplating law school or some other costly graduate or undergraduate program ...because you are *hoping* it will increase your marketability and earning power, do the research and back up that hope with the facts. I'm not totally against student loans, especially if they're used to train for in-demand careers like nursing, teaching, information technology or engineering. If not, do *a cost-benefit analysis* before pursuing a plan that will laden your future with massive debt. No matter what path you plan to pursue, look for an intelligent low cost way to finance the pursuit of your dream.

Faith to Find a Job

*"Trust in the Lord with all your heart and lean not to your own understanding, **in all your ways acknowledge Him** and He will direct your path." (Proverb 3:5-6)*

If you are a recent college graduate try to address the issue of your marketability in practical and affordable ways. Do what you can to find that base line good job perhaps at an organization that will finance a graduate degree through a tuition reimbursement program. If you're facing a mountain of student loan debt, humble yourself and seek God's direction for your life. A debt that seems like a Goliath problem to you ...is a small thing to the Father. **He can provide!**

Finally understand that Proverbs 3:5-6 quoted just above is telling us to *pray* before we develop a vision. Pray before we make a decision. Pray as we formulate a plan. Pray before we put a plan in action. And all along the way, listen for God's direction and wisdom to guide you. If you seek the Lord's will and way...He will guide you.

Reality Check: *One of the biggest mistakes people make, is refusing to hear the wisdom of those who love them but oppose their dream. Never fear the truth in love. God is the truth in love. No one can talk you out of your dreams. However, those who love you will want you to pursue them in a way that takes into account the uncertainties that may be up ahead. It's only wisdom to formulate a viable Plan B.*

Chapter 16

The Favor of God

*"My soul magnifies the Lord,
And my spirit has rejoiced in God my Savior.
For He has regarded the lowly state of His maidservant;"
(Luke 2: 46-48)*

One day when I was about eight years old, I walked into my Sunday school classroom, and there, displayed prominently on the teacher's desk, was one of those commercially packaged Christmas stocking stuffed with lots of candies and little toys. I grew up one of six children and our modest family life rarely included extravagances like that wonderful Christmas treat. So just seeing it there, was enough to get me excited. Any way as soon as the class settled down, my Sunday school teacher explained that we were going to have a *holiday raffle* and the student with the winning ticket would get to take the Christmas stocking home.

From the moment my teacher handed it to me, I knew...*I knew* I had the winning ticket. It wasn't a hope. It wasn't a strong desire. It was a *knowing* that God put in my spirit. John 3:27 states that a *" man can receive nothing, unless it has been given to him from heaven."* And that day when my teacher read the winning numbers...*the numbers that were on my ticket,* I knew...*I knew* that I received a special gift from Heaven.

Thank you Lord... for making a little girl that didn't feel special at all... feel special that day!

Faith to Find a Job

I love that memory, that kiss on the cheek from God. It's my earliest recollection of receiving **divine favor.** When I think back on that experience and *why I was selected*, I know that it was by the **grace (unmerited favor) of God** and *not* because I was being rewarded for anything that I had done. If so, I'm sure the Lord would have tied the harvest to the seed. In any case, that's the first thing I want you to understand about the favor of God *...that it's about God's goodness and power and not about what we deserve.* If you are believing God to bless you with a good job then you need to understand *grace* and *divine favor* in a profound way. If you don't, feelings of unworthiness can rise up and rob you of this blessed hope. Indeed, *if you are looking for a job by faith then you need to understand that the favor of God consummates the selection process.* After you've polished up your resume and sowed it into the job market, the favor of God is what will move the right person to pick it out of a stack of resumes and say after your interview, *"That is exactly who I'm looking for!"*

*"For **they did not gain possession of the land by their own sword, nor did their own arm save them** but it was your right hand, Your arm and the light of Your countenance, **because you favored them**." (Psalm 44:3)*

During my last job search, I probably repeated Psalm 44:3 to myself more than a hundred times. That good word from the Psalms assured me that my confidence was not in my qualifications or lack of recent work experience in my field. No, I would gain possession of the land (a good job) because God could open any door and establish me. And He was going to open a door and establish me *...because **He** favored me!*

Faith to Find a Job

That was honestly my faith. God's grace was sufficient and I believed it was all I needed. God had a provision for me, because I believe He has a provision for each of His children. *Neither the state of the economy nor **my competition** for a job, would in any way diminish God's ability to provide for me.* And understand, those things will in no way diminish God's ability to provide for you. No one can receive *anything,* unless it has been given to him from Heaven. Let that good word from the gospel of John, assure you that no one can take the job that God has for you. You don't have to be anxious about a particular position or anything else. If it's God's provision for you...you will *gain possession of the land* and no amount of competition or anything will be able to stop you.

*Now am I trying to win **the favor of men**, or of God? Do I seek to please men? If I were still seeking popularity with men, I should not be a bond servant of Christ (the Messiah). Galatians 1:10*

Sometimes a classified *job ad* can seem like an extravagant Christmas treat. It appears to offer everything we've been looking for ...everything we hope to find in a job. That is how I felt one Sunday afternoon as I read a new internet listing for the type of job I was looking for. Almost all the experience they wanted, *I had.* And the salary range exceeded my expectation. So I promptly emailed my resume and cover letter over to the company and within three days I found myself seated in the elegant lobby of an upscale real estate investment firm *waiting to be interviewed.* As I sat there waiting, I reveled in the posh decor and eclectic luxury of the artwork that surrounded me and thought that it was an especially beautiful place to work.

Faith to Find a Job

My interview with the HR Manager went extremely well. She was warm and excited about my qualifications. Moreover, I felt like I put forth the right balance of confidence and humility because within a half hour, she was escorting me to another floor to interview with two individuals that I would potentially be working with. However, as the HR Manager introduced me to the senior staff person, the countenance on her face plummeted as soon as she saw me, and I could see that she didn't want to work with me. Still I smiled and pressed in and tried my best to reveal how nice I was and how easy-going my nature tends to be. Nevertheless, in spite of all the gracious words that passed between us, I knew...*I knew* when I left that place that I was not her choice for that job.

On the way home I struggled to release my hopes for that position. I wasn't mad at God in the least bit... and my faith that I would find a good job, was not diminished at all. The Word says that the just shall walk by faith and not by sight and that the Lord will choose our inheritance for us. For that reason, I never name and claim a position, but I always seek God's sovereign will for my life. God's provision, whatever it may be, I trust will be good and sufficient. Still, it wasn't easy and it didn't seem fair. We were two women about the same age...why didn't she like me? How could she make up her mind about me the instant, she saw me. The answer was at the heart of my spirit...the notion, that if we had been of the *same race* perhaps she would not have rejected me so easily.

*"Coming to Him as to a living stone, **rejected** indeed by **men, but chosen by God and precious**..." (I Peter 2:4)*

Faith to Find a Job

In all likelihood, before you are selected for a job, you will be rejected more than a few times...at least that was my experience! Aside from not getting *any* response to an application, I think being out right rejected is one of the most painful and discouraging aspects of job hunting. In fact, it will erode your faith if you don't stand against it. I can't tell you how many times I got a call from an employment agency, when not five minutes into the conversation...right after I explained why I didn't have any dates on my resume, the agent said to me (like she was talking to an inanimate object that had no brain or feelings), *"Oh! I can't do anything with you!"*

"Really!" I would **say** defiantly... *as soon as I hung up the phone.* Then, in full assurance that what I was about to speak was 100% true, I would counter the negative words that had just been spoken to me by saying, *"I will not get a good job because you or anyone else believes in me. I won't even get a job because I believe in myself. I will get a good job because I believe in God! He can open any door. Blessing me with a good job is a small thing to God. You"* (I'd say thinking of the rude employment agent that had just dismissed me) *"will not have the last word in my life."*

Time and again, I made those *confessions of faith,* and each time I meant every word. I refused to think hopeless thoughts, and I was not going to let someone who did not know the power of God characterize me as *worthless.* I'll say it again, *if you don't stand against it, rejection will erode your faith.* So fight the good fight of faith... *reject rejection* and choose to believe the hope and promises in God's word.

Faith to Find a Job

Rejected by men, but chosen by God and precious... Those words from I Peter 2:4 are some of my favorites, because they speak of the awesome ways that God can make a difference in our lives. God is wonderfully able to turn a negative into a positive, a curse into a blessing (Deuteronomy 11:28)...a rejection into acceptance.

Believing God for His divine favor can be such a refreshing experience. When God enters the equation, we don't have to fear the way we've been treated in the past, nor do we have to worry that we will be *victimized* by *racism, sexism, age discrimination*...or any other way that *favoritism* seeks to exclude us.

> *"Teacher, we know that You say and teach rightly, and You do not show **personal favoritism**, but teach the way of God in truth..." (Luke 20:21)*

Rejection is not from God so don't swallow it. It's a bitter poison! Spew it out! It's not the final word. The Word of God is the final word in your life. So hold fast to your **confessions of faith** that are based on God's promises. Psalm 44:3 describes how the children of Israel prevailed in their battle for the Promise Land, but it also describes our promised victory. You will not find a decent job because you believe in yourself or because anyone else believes in you. *You will find a good job because you believe in God* and His ability to open a door through His divine favor!

> *You have granted me life and favor, and Your care has preserved my spirit. (Job 10:12)*

Faith to Find a Job

Reality Check: Employment agencies only get paid if the candidate they refer is hired. For that reason, they seek out what they perceive to be the finest candidate for a job. During my last job search, I was able to get several really good interviews through employment agencies, however for people who have a blemish in their work history or a special circumstance to explain, employment agencies are generally not the best way to go.

Chapter 17

I Believe... Therefore, I Speak

*"**Then Joshua spoke to the Lord** in the day when the Lord delivered up the Amorites...."**Sun, stand still over Gibeon; and Moon in the Valley of Aijalon.**" **So the sun stood still** in the midst of the heaven, and did not hasten to go down for the whole day. And there has been no day like that, before it or after it, that **the Lord heeded the voice of a man**..."*
(Joshua 10:12, 13 and 14)

When negative words were spoken about me, I countered them with positive confessions of faith. The Bible teaches that words have creative power, so I used my faith in that biblical doctrine to speak positive words of faith into my life and job search. Confessions of faith or positive confessions are acts of faith much like prayer. Faith is a belief in an unseen reality. Most people believe in the unseen reality of God, so that is a degree of faith. Many people also believe that the unseen reality of God, can effect control and alter natural and physical conditions. For that reason, many of us act on our faith by praying. We petition God through prayer and then hope that He will respond by effecting physical and natural conditions. Prayer then is an act of faith.

Positive confessions are acts of faith that are based in an extensive biblical doctrine that teaches that the spiritual realm responds to our words and authority and as a result physical and natural conditions can be altered and effected *by what we say.*

Jesus spoke to dead men, and they came back to life. He spoke to the wind and the waves, and they obeyed Him. Furthermore, to demonstrate this very principle, He taught in Mark 11:22-24, Jesus spoke to a vibrant fig tree that appeared to be bearing fruit and the next day when His disciples saw the tree, it had withered away from its roots. *Be imitators of God as dear children (Ephesians 5:1).*

> *"God, who gives life to the dead **and calls those things which do not exist as though they did...**" (Romans 4:17)*

Confessions of Faith

Confessions of faith are promises and positive words based in the Word of God that we speak in faith over our lives or over the lives of others. As we speak our confessions, we believe we are going to see them manifest. For instance, if you want to see God's power divinely intervene in your job search, **you might confess**, *I can do all things through Christ, who strengthens me...I can find a good job!* Or *I am blessed and highly favored, I am favored above all the other candidates for the job.*

When I first began making positive confessions, I thought the idea was a bit silly. Still, I kept hearing about how effective it was, so *I just made up my mind to do it.* First, I compiled a list of confessions from the Word of God that I wanted to see manifested in my life. Then, I added some things that I was believing for and had the faith to receive. Finally, I began speaking my confessions out loud as a part of my private prayer time. It did not take long, maybe a couple of weeks, and I began to see some of the things that I was confessing come to pass. Seeing some of my confessions manifest, fueled my faith and helped me to believe that my whole list of confessions would eventually manifest.

These days I see my list of positive confessions not only as an extension of prayer, but also as a form of spiritual warfare. My confessions of faith build a hedge of protection around me and my loved ones. I gain and maintain victories and war against my spiritual adversary, by speaking words of faith like the following:

> ➢ *No weapon formed against me shall prosper, and every tongue that rises against me in judgment, I will prove to be wrong.*

> ➢ *Let lying lips be put to silence, which speak insolent things proudly and contemptuously against the righteous. Let lying lips be put to silence, which speak insolent things proudly and contemptuously against me!"*

*"For assuredly, I say to you whoever **says** to this mountain, be removed and cast into the sea and does not doubt in his heart, but believes that those things he **says** will be done, he will have whatever he **says**!*

Therefore, I say to you whatever things you ask when you pray, believe that you receive them and you will have them."
(Mark 11:23-24)

Just as faith is important to prayer, faith is also important to making positive confessions and seeing a manifestation of those words in your life. As you read this book and study the Word of God, if you see a scripture or a promise that you would like to see manifested in your life, personalize it and speak it out loud. Then, have faith that God will heed your voice, like he heeded the voice of Joshua, and bring your confession to pass.

> *You will also declare a thing,*
> *And it will be established for you;*
> *So light will shine on your ways. (Job 22:28)*

Hinderances to Our Faith and Confessions

In Mark 11: 23, Jesus tells us that *if we believe the things we say will be done, then we will have whatever we say.* That statement seems like a perfect way to end this teaching on the power of positive confession. But the Lord does not end his teaching there. Instead he goes on to tell us something else important to seeing our prayers answered. Jesus goes on to say, *"if you have anything against anyone, forgive them."* The Lord says something similar after *the Model Prayer ...forgive or the Father will not forgive you* (Matthew 6:14-15). If we are filled with bitterness and un-forgiveness than, we are in debt to the Lord. Our prayers will go unanswered, and our positive confessions will not come to pass. In fact, I think there are basically three things that rob our words of power and negate our positive confessions, and they are:

1. *Canceling your positive confession with negative words,*
2. *Speaking evil words against other people,*
3. *Holding on to offences and refusing to forgive.*

Do not cancel your positive confessions with negative words. Just as you need to counter damaging words that others speak about you, understand you need to *watch your own words* to make sure you don't negate your confessions of faith. For instance, if you are confessing in your prayer that you are blessed and highly favored, and you are favored above all the other candidates for the job. Later, don't tell your friend, *'Nobody likes me ...I'll never find a job!'*

Which is the faith confession you really believe? Which ones will manifest, the words you spoke in your prayer, or the ones you said to your friend?

> *"Let not a slanderer be established in the earth;"*
> *(Psalm 140:11)*

Speaking evil against others will rob your words of power. Gossiping, criticizing, and lying are just some of the ways you can cut yourself off from the life and power of God (Psalm 110). *Devil* means *slanderer,* so understand, God is not going to empower a devil's mouth. God wants us to be a blessing to others (Genesis 12:1-3). He is not going to manifest a curse or words that will harm others. And if you're double-minded on this point, don't expect to get anything from the Lord. (James 1:7-8)

Make up your mind that you are only going to talk positively about yourself, your circumstances and others. Confess the sins of your mouth and repent, and then ask God to help you sanctify the words of your mouth. Do these things and you will see the words that you speak in faith come to life.

> *"Seeing that we have a great High Priest who has passed through the heavens, Jesus the Son of God, let us hold fast our*

confession. For we do not have a High Priest who cannot sympathize with our weakness, but was in all points tempted as we are, yet without sin. Let us therefore come boldly to the **throne of grace**, *that we may obtain* **mercy** *and find* **grace** *to help in time of need." (Hebrew 4:14-16)*

Confessions of Faith for a Successful Job Hunt

Following are a few of the positive confessions to enhance your **faith to find a job:**

➢ *I shall decree a thing, and it shall be established. I believe! Therefore, I speak. I do not doubt in my heart, I will have what I say! Praise God!*

➢ *I shall bless the Lord at all times, His praise shall continually be in my mouth. No evil communication will proceed out of my mouth, but only words that edify the hearers. God has set a guard over my mouth, and He keeps watch over the door of my lips. I am not a liar. I am not a gossip. I am not a devil.*

➢ *The beauty of the Lord is upon me. God is establishing the work of my hands for me. Yes, God is establishing the work of my hands for me. Nothing is impossible for God. Blessing me with a good job is a small thing to God.*

➢ *I can do all things through Christ, who strengthens me. I can conduct a successful job search. I can find a good job. I am a diligent worker. I will inherit the promises of God through faith and patience.*

➢ *I am not the victim of racism, sexism, age discrimination or any form of favoritism. No man shall be able to stand against me all the days of my life. As the Lord was with Moses, He is also with me.*

Faith to Find a Job

> ➢ *One of my job applications will fall on good ground and bring forth the harvest of a job offer. If I seek a good job...I will find one.*

> ➢ *I am blessed and highly favored. The favor of God surrounds me like a shield. I am favored above all the other candidates for the job. I will get a good job because God favors me. Now is the set time to favor me! (Praise God!)*

> ➢ *The Lord is my shepherd, I shall not want. My God shall supply all of my need according to his riches in glory by Christ Jesus. I have begun to prosper, and I will continue to prosper until I have become very...very prosperous. I have been redeemed from the curse of the law. I have been redeemed from the curse of poverty, sickness and disease. I have been redeemed from the curse of unemployment.*

> ➢ *Let lying lips be put to silence, which speak insolent things proudly and contemptuously against the righteous. Let lying lips be put to silence, which speak insolent things proudly and contemptuously against me. No weapon formed against me shall prosper and every tongue that rises against me in judgment I shall prove to be in the wrong.*

Chapter 18

God's Plan for Good Success

*"And therefore the Lord [earnestly] waits [expecting, looking, and longing] to be gracious to you; and therefore **He lifts Himself up**, that He may have mercy on you and show loving kindness to you. **For the Lord is a God of justice.** Blessed (happy, fortunate, to be envied are all those who [earnestly] wait for Him, who expect and look and long for Him, [for **His victory, His favor, His love**, His peace, His joy and His matchless unbroken, companionship]." (Isaiah 30:18 Amplified Bible)*

The Favor Factor by *Kate McVeigh* was the first book I read on the favor of God, and it was a divine revelation. Until I read that book, it never occurred to me that God had anything so wonderful in store for me and the people He loves. The woman who wrote the book described how as a child growing up, she was rejected and ridiculed because she was a *special ed* student. She said the kids at her school regularly laughed at her, called her names and as a result, she grew up lacking confidence and self-esteem. Then one summer when she was still in high school, she joined a church and got saved while the pastor was teaching a series on the favor of God. The revelation that *God loved her and could **make** others like her and treat her well* was something that spoke to her deepest need. What she lacked most... what she needed most, was something that God could give her. So she took hold of the promises **by faith,** and it changed her life *almost immediately.*

"Rejoice, highly favored one, the Lord is with you*; blessed are you among women!" (Luke 1:28)*

Faith to Find a Job

When the summer was over, McVeigh said she returned to her high school walking in faith that she was blessed and highly favored by the Lord. That faith, she said, changed the way she saw herself and the way others saw and treated her. Not only did her classmates and others deal with her in greater respect, but she said everyone, including McVeigh herself, was astounded by the confidence and courage that her new Faith brought to her life.

Jesus told people, "*according to your faith so be it,*" but understand, that means our faith can work for ...or against us. If we have faith that people won't like us...they won't. If we have faith that we are not the best candidate for a job...we won't be. However, if we embrace the Faith that we are blessed and highly favored and that the Lord is with us ...like McVeigh, we can restructure our confidence and experience with the world.

"Do not be afraid...for you have found favor with God..."
(Luke 1:30)

A job offer will be extended to you because you are favored above all the other candidates for the job. Does that statement sound familiar? It's from the first chapter of this book... *it's how we started this faith journey.* To a job hunter, the favor of God speaks to our deepest need. What we need most...someone to favor us and offer us a job, is something that God can give us. What we can't make happen for ourselves **God can make** happen for us and that is essentially the promise in this next verse of scripture:

*"And **God is able to make** all grace (every favor and earthly blessing) come to you in abundance, so that you may always and*

Faith to Find a Job

under all circumstances and whatever the need be self-sufficient [possessing enough to require no aid or support and furnished in abundance for every good work and charitable donation". (II Corinthians 9:8 - Amplified Bible)

The Amplified version of II Corinthians 9:8 is another scripture verse that I have meditated and probably *confessed out loud* a thousand times. I love it because it is so rich with potential to change our lives. *And we can have every single bit of what is promised if we meditate on this verse until it becomes a part of our faith.* This scripture tells me that *God wants* to furnish everything we need *in abundance,* so we have everything we need to be *self-sufficient.* It is what God wants. He wants us to have good paying jobs...*okay!* He does not want us to be poor and needy...God wants us to be *self-sufficient! Praise God!*

According to our faith *so be it...remember!* So we need to meditate on II Corinthians 9:8, confess it out loud and let the wealth of the revelation become our faith! Once we believe it, we can start expecting to experience the abounding grace. What is more, look at what the scripture says.... **God is able to make favor abound toward us** ...it's not up to us to make it happen. We don't have to try to impress people or sell ourselves to win favor...God is able to make it happen. *Why?* So we will have everything that we need! So we can be self-sufficient! So we can overflow and abound to good works! *Praise God!*

" I will bless you, and make your name great, and you shall be a blessing." (Genesis 12:2)

Okay...here is the power point again: *We can have every single bit of what is promised in scripture if we meditate on it until it becomes our faith.* Understand, the lessons in this book are just inspirational sermons that will fade away if we allow them to. However, if we work our faith through meditation... the words of God will become to us like **a beautiful well-crafted sailboat that will carry us securely to our destination**.

Go back and look at the Introduction to this book. Read again that my last job search took 10 months and my testimony is that *I never got discouraged.* My testimony is that my faith, like a well-crafted sailboat carried me securely to my intended destination... an offer for a good job. The key to remaining positive and hopeful was that I *continuously* meditated on inspirational sermons and scriptures that magnified God and His promises over my circumstance. My immediate results and circumstances were not my focus. In fact, when my circumstances were contrary to what my Faith was telling me...I confessed, to my circumstances, *"I don't believe you. I don't receive your message of discouragement."*

"Get behind Me, Satan! For it is written. "You shall worship the Lord your God, and Him only you shall serve." (Luke 4:8)

Meditating, speaking, and obeying scripture is the plan for **good success** that God laid out for us in **Joshua 1:8-9.** Hundreds of years after God dictated His success plan to Joshua, we see *Jesus working it* to gain victory over the devil. In Luke 4:4 the Lord is hungering and wrestling with the temptation to do something other than *rest in His Faith.* Nevertheless, the Lord overcame the devil's temptation by speaking faith that was rooted in the Word of God, *"It is written,"* Jesus told the devil, *"Man shall not live by bread alone but by every word of God."*

Faith to Find a Job

In case you didn't know it, Jesus was quoting Deuteronomy 8:3, a scripture that was applicable to his situation, words that were written hundreds of years before he was born.

> *"So He humbled you, allowed you to hunger, and fed you with manna which you did not know nor did your fathers know, that He might make you know that* **man shall not live by bread alone, but man lives by every word that proceeds from the mouth of the Lord***." (Deuteronomy 8:2-3)*

When Jesus was hungering in the wilderness, he countered his negative circumstance by meditating and speaking Deuteronomy 8:2-3. That scripture told him that He was being tested, explained why, and gave him the answer he needed to pass the test. Jesus was in that situation tasting hunger, poverty and crisis...because those who would believe on Him would taste the same things.

The Lord's test in the wilderness is an example for us. He didn't panic when he was in crisis. He didn't believe the dire nature of His circumstances. Instead, he worked his faith *in the scriptures.* Jesus needed a miracle provision in the wilderness, but he knew, The Father had provided a *miracle provision in the wilderness* for Hagar (Genesis 21: 14-21). And for forty years, God miraculously fed millions of people in the wilderness (Exodus 16:11-19). Jesus was working his Faith in a God, who could handle dire circumstances. *'Get behind me Satan...I don't believe you.* Jesus said essentially, *'I don't receive your message of fear and death. God is well able to provide for me the way He provided for others. My faith,'* the Lord said to the devil, *'is that God will sustain me miraculously the way His Word promises He will.'*

Faith to Find a Job

"Then the devil left Him, and behold, angels came and ministered to Him." (Matthew 4:11)

Working our faith and living by the word of God means that we *don't* live by the news reports about the economy and the job market. It means we *don't* live by our fears related to what happened to us in the past. Even advice from well-meaning friends and family can be a hindrance to our faith if it falls short of what God's Word promises. Working our faith means that we believe and act on what the Bible says about our situation...that is God's formula for *good success*.

*"This book of the Law shall not depart from your **mouth**, but you shall **meditate** in it day and night, that you may observed to **do** according to all that is written in it. For **then you will make your way prosperous** and then you will have **good success**. Have I not commanded you? Be strong and of good courage, do not be afraid, nor be dismayed, for the Lord your God is with you wherever you go." (Joshua 1:8-9)*

In this verse of scripture God is telling us how to work **the Faith He has given us...** speak the word of God, meditate on it, and obey it. If we will do that then like Joshua and Jesus, we too can have *good success*.

I cannot offer anyone a formula for success better than that of Joshua 1:8, *but I can testify that it works.* Understand, *what you believe is little "f" faith.* Anything can influence your little "f" faith. The devil can contaminate it. The nightly news that says unemployment is up and the economy is down, can formulate it. Your perceived lack of qualifications or the fear of being victimized by racism or age discrimination can contaminate your little "f" faith. However, like the woman we read about at the beginning of this chapter, God is offering you a different Faith. He is calling you to live by your *big "F" faith...the doctrine and teachings of the Word of God.* Little "f" faith doesn't figure God into the equation but big "F" Faith tells us that God is in control. Meditating, speaking and obeying the Word of God is the way to **make your way prosperous** and bring about **good success.** That is big "F" faith and that is the faith you need to find a job!

*"This is the word of the Lord to Zerubbabel: **Not by might nor by power, but by My Spirit**, says the Lord of hosts. Who are you, O great mountain? Before Zerubbabel you shall become a plain! And he shall bring forth the capstone with shouts of 'Grace, grace to it!"* (Zechariah 4: 6-7)

Who are you O great mountain of unemployment and lack? You shall become like a plain before the men and women who believe God's Word. They shall prosper in spite of you...they will bring forth God's victory by His grace...by shouting Grace...grace to you! That's how we work our Faith...we speak the Word of God into our circumstance the way Jesus did. Victory by grace is not rooted in our power, but comes about by the Spirit of the Lord. God's Word is *His Spirit!* (John 1:1 and John 6:63).

*"For though we walk according to the flesh, we do not war according to the flesh. For the weapons of our warfare are not carnal but mighty in God for pulling down strongholds, **casting down arguments** and every high thing that exalts itself against the knowledge of God, **bringing every thought into captivity** to the obedience of Christ..."*
(2 Corinthians 10:4-5)

Faith to Find a Job

Reality Check: *If we embrace the faith, that we are blessed and highly favored, we can restructure our confidence and experience with the world.*

Chapter 19

Divine Favor for the Humble

"Therefore, I say to you, whatever things you ask when you pray,
believe that you receive them, and you will have them.
And.... But...." *(Mark 11:24-26)*

When my daughter was a little girl it seemed like she was always working on some special acquisition. A new set of bobbles for her hair, a new outfit for one of her Barbie dolls, or the latest fruit flavored lip balm were some of the things that were routinely on her *must have* list. After a while, I noticed that my daughter became very strategic in the way she approached me about the things that she wanted. She would say, *'Mommy can you buy me a new outfit for Barbie?'* To which I would generally reply, *'Not today Honey... it's not in the budget!'*

However, my daughter would always press in with, *'When Mommy? When will it be in the budget?'* To which I would generally reply with an answer like, *'Well...**if you keep your room clean,** and you keep up with your schoolwork, maybe ...next payday?'*

What I began to notice is that once my daughter got a *promise* from me ...*next payday?* She would walk away *happy,* as though she already had what she was asking for. That is because I was very careful to keep *my promises* to her ...and she knew it! Believe it or not these grace encounters with my daughter can teach us quite a bit about how God answers prayer. Psalm 37:4 states, *"Delight yourself in the Lord and He will give you the desires of your heart."* That promise almost seems like a blank check... but it is not, because the promise is really contingent upon us delighting ourselves in the Lord!

Cultivate a quality relationship with the Lord. Work the Joshua 1:8 plan for good success. That is what Psalm 37:4 really means. Spend time with the Lord in prayer. Get to know Him through His Word, and when you do that, you will find out what my daughter found out about me, that God is very careful to keep **His promises.** In fact, once we have *His promise*, like my daughter, we can walk around happy and in faith that payday *is* coming.

> **"God resists the proud,**
> **but gives grace to the humble "**
> *(2 Peter 5:5)*

Let me add to your understanding of believing and receiving from the Lord. If my daughter had left her socks in the middle of the floor during the time that she was waiting on my next payday and her new Barbie doll outfit, even though she was supposed to keep her room clean, if she wasn't around, I would probably just pick up her socks and put them away without saying a word. Her imperfection was not a deal changer. However, if she did something much more egregious like sassing me or her teacher...that was a **deal changer**. I was *not* going to reward that kind of behavior.

More than anything else, job hunters need *the favor of God to consummate the selection process,* so it is a good idea to understand as much as you can about God's grace and favor. For instance, you can pray and ask God to give you favor in your job search, but *if you have a problem with pride*, the verse quoted above will let you know, God is resisting you. In fact, if you are proud and arrogant chances are nobody, not even God, wants to do you a favor.

"Therefore, humble yourselves under the mighty hand of God that He may exalt you in due time...." (2 Peter 5:6)

The scripture quoted here tells us that humility is an important aspect of cultivating the grace of God. So, let's think about *humility*, what it is, and what it is not. First, humility is not putting yourself down, and it is not low-self-esteem. *In fact, unlike pride, humility is really not about you. It is about acknowledging your need for God's help and guidance in your life.* A proud person thinks he can figure it out himself. He thinks he can achieve his goals through his own efforts. If he manages to accomplish anything, he compares himself to others who have not succeeded in the same manner. A proud person's accomplishments lead him to magnify his own talent and abilities and his failures contribute directly to his lack of self-esteem. Whether you feel good or bad about yourself... pride may be the root of your problem.

"Most assuredly, I say to you, the Son can do nothing of Himself, but what He sees the Father do, for whatever He does, the Son also does in like manner. I can of Myself do nothing... (John 5:19 and 30)

If Jesus said that he could do nothing without God, then understand *we* will not be able to accomplish anything apart from God, a humble person knows that. A person walking in humility looks to Heaven and magnifies the Lord and what God can do and has done in his life. Humility prays in earnest, *'God, I need you! I cannot do this without you! I do not trust my own wisdom and abilities to accomplish anything, so show me the way and give me your favor.* Humility makes a connection with the Holy Spirit and His favor and blessing. So much so, that when the blessing manifests ...when the job offer comes, humility thanks God and praises Him for the blessing.

Reality Check: *If you believed you received a good job, a blessing, when you prayed, then you can rejoice in faith that your pay day is coming. And as you wait, walk in humility expecting God's divine favor to open the door and consummate the selection process with a job offer.*

Faith to Find a Job

Chapter 20

The Supernatural... The Job Offer

*...whatever things you ask when **you pray, believe that you receive them**, and you will have them. Mark 11:24*

Faith starts when we pray. This book is my testimony that for ten months, I believed God would bless me with a good job. That faith started when I prayed, the day I started my job search. I also believed that God would give me the resume and cover letter that I needed to get the job He had for me. That faith started when I prayed, and it continued to stoke my confidence as I worked to develop first rate employment documents. Then as I searched for a job, like the *parable of the sower*, I also believed that one of my job applications would fall on good ground and bring forth the harvest of job interviews and eventually a job offer. Finally, I used my faith and imagination to envision God working behind the scenes establishing the work of my hands for me. And in the end when I got the job, as you are about to find out, it too was a test of my faith ...a job offer wrapped in the supernatural as a gift from God.

Works of the Flesh

"You have become estranged from Christ. you who attempt to be justified by the law; you have fallen from grace. (Galatians 5:4)

One night I had a dream that I was trying to climb a thick *maritime rope* that was hanging from the sky. With all my strength, and all my might, I tried to climb and climb that rope. You know how dreams are? I was sleeping but *I wasn't resting* because my soul was involved in this frustrating endeavor. I do not know why I had to climb that rope, but there was no giving up. At the top of the rope was a better life, so I struggled and struggled to climb. *Then,* out of nowhere, a giant pair of scissors appeared and cut the rope. As I watched it crumbled to the ground, so my hope crumbled with it.

When I woke up from that dream, I knew right away that the rope wasn't from God. Then the Holy Spirit revealed that the dream was about the *works of the flesh.* As painful as that dream had been...it seemed to characterize my greatest struggle at that time in my life. I thought that if I could just overcome my sinful nature, God could bless me, and I could escape to a better life. However, the Lord revealed that my real life struggle had nothing to do with His grace, but everything to do with the devil's delight in frustrating me.

Satanic perfection, the Holy Spirit revealed, *is based on a flawless performance.* It's a legalistic concept; a carrot on a rope that the devil dangles over our head and in our face to make us run faster and jump higher. It is a wicked device aimed at frustrating us and inspiring us to give up... because in the end, there is no real prize.

"Come... Let's build a great city and a tower that reaches to the skies---a monument to our greatness! But the Lord came down to see the city and the tower ...and that ended the building of the city." (Genesis 11:4, 5,)

Sometimes a job search can seem like a carrot on a rope that is dangling over your head. If you can just grab hold of the carrot, a good job, you can escape to a better life. So, you run faster, jump higher, network, and send out more resumes. You do everything you can, but much as you try; there is no prize in the end. You tell yourself, *'God helps those who help themselves.'* Then you convince yourself that you are up to the challenge and giving up is not an option! You do everything you can to keep yourself *psyched up* because you are on the verge of giving up ...because it's just *so hard.*

*"Cursed is the man who trust in man, **and makes flesh his strength**, whose heart departs from the Lord." "Blessed is the man who trust in the Lord, and whose hope is the Lord." (Jeremiah 17: 5 and 7)*

*Feelings of **lust** and **frustration** are the best indications that you have gotten out of faith and into **works of the flesh**. Frustration is the express lane on the highway to discouragement and defeat! So if you are wrangling with frustration, understand...your faith is rooted in the process of looking for a job and your ability to make the process work for you. On some level you believe that if you work at the process right or long enough...it will pay off in the end. However, if you have been at it for a while but the process isn't working for you...you might want to ask yourself, **where is God in your struggle?***

Nowhere in the Bible does it state that, God helps those who help themselves, but the Word does state, *"Those who seek the Lord shall not lack any good thing." (Psalm 34:10)* And it also states, *"As long as he sought the Lord, the Lord made him to prosper!" (2 Chronicles 26:5)*

"The godly will inherit the land and live their forever. The godly offer good counsel; they know what is right from wrong.

Faith to Find a Job

They fill their hearts with God's law, so they will never slip from his path!" (Psalm 37:29-31)

I have heard it said that *if you do not have a full-time job, then looking for a full-time job should be your full-time job. But I do not entirely agree with that statement. If you do not have a full-time job, then looking for a full-time job should be one of your top priorities...but it is a mistake to make it your number one priority.* Jesus said, *seek first the kingdom of God and His righteousness, and all these things shall be added to you."* (Matthew 6:33). That is not just a prescription for the Christian way to pursue your provision, no... the alternative, seeking things first, will leave you fearful, frustrated and wrangling with poverty.

"All things are lawful but all things are not profitable. All things are lawful, but I will not come under the power of anything." (I Corinthian 6: 12)

Employment listings, even on the major job sites, do not change that significantly from day to day. So when I was *in the middle* of my job search, I limited the time I spent searching for a job to a few hours a day, for two but no more than three days a week. Even then, if I felt myself getting frustrated or lustful for results, I immediately turned off my computer and refocused on building my faith in the promises of God. When I felt frustrated, it was honestly more profitable for me to nourish my *Faith to find a job*, then it was for me to search for a job.

When frustration began to invade my spirit, instead of combing the web for a job lead, I prayed, listened to teaching tapes on divine favor or meditated and confessed scriptures. Sometimes I listened to gospel music or did something else to relax and **rest** from the process of looking for a job. Understand, I spent quite a bit of time searching for a job, but I know I put more time and effort into nourishing my Faith to find that job.

> *"For thus says the Lord God, the Holy One of Israel:* **In returning and rest you shall be saved.** *In quietness and confidence shall be your strength." (Isaiah 30:15)*

Do not get me wrong, it's right and necessary for us to spend a considerable amount of time searching for a job, but don't come under the power of the process. As soon as you feel frustrated or sense that you are lusting for results, back off from *your efforts* and the process of looking for a job. Do more to build and nourish your faith and to remind yourself that God is behind the scene establishing the work of your hands for you. Much as we try, we cannot make it happen...but the Lord can.

> *"Therefore, since a promise remains of entering His rest, let us fear lest any of you seem to have come short of it. For* **indeed the gospel was preached to us as well as to them; but the word which they heard did not profit them, not being mixed with faith** *in those who heard it.* **For we who believed do enter that rest....**" *(Hebrews 4:1-3)*

Entering God's Rest

Years ago, I bought an anointed teaching tape series called *God's Waiting Room* by Pastor Mack Hammond. In it, Pastor Hammond shares a divine revelation that changed my life and elevated my faith on numerous occasions to receive a manifestation of the promise I was waiting on. The essence of this teaching is, that when we are in God's waiting room waiting on God's promises to be manifest, the Lord is not the one delaying the breakthrough ...*we are!* Indeed, Pastor Hammond said that God is waiting for us to mix the gospel, with our faith and then to enter His rest. When God sees us resting in our Faith, His promise will come forth. That mixing of our faith with the Gospel, with the promises in God's Word, for those of us who believe, Hebrews 4:3 is essentially saying, we will come to a time and place where we will rest in our faith believing our prayer is answered even though we cannot yet see the substance of it.

Now faith is the substance of things hoped for the evidence of things not seen. Hebrews 11:2

The Set Time to Favor Me Had Come

Remember a few chapters back when I was talking about that disappointing interview. I saw a posting for what I thought was the perfect job and within three days of submitting my resume, I was sitting in a beautiful office downtown interviewing for that job. However, as I was introduced to the senior staff person at the beginning of the second phase of the interview process, the countenance on her face plummeted as soon as she saw me. I could see that she didn't want to work with me and in the end, I did not get that job.

That day and that experience was very hard on me. I knew I was not going to get the job when I left the interview. And on the way home I found myself struggling to accept the rejection that I knew was coming. I was disappointed and hurt, but the faith that I had been building since the beginning of my job search would not let me cry, complain, or give up my hope. When I reached home, for the first time in the ten months, I think *I could have* opened the door to discouragement. But instead, I sat down on my bed, picked up my Bible and looked up. I needed the Holy Spirit to speak to me and He did. Within minutes of opening my Bible, inexplicably I was reading this verse:

*"Therefore, humble yourselves under the mighty hand of God that **He may exalt you in due time**, casting all your care upon Him, for He cares for you. Be sober, be vigilant, because your adversary the devil walks about like a roaring lion, seeking whom he may devour. Resist him, steadfast in the faith, knowing that **the same sufferings are experienced by your brotherhood in the world.** But may the God of all grace who called us to His eternal glory by Christ Jesus, **after you have suffered a while**, perfect, **establish,** strengthen, and **settle you**. To Him be the glory and the dominion forever and ever. Amen*
. (I Peter 5: 6-11)

As I read this passage of scripture, the words **establish, strengthen, and settle you** popped off the page and started burning in my soul. As I read the passage again, I knew the Lord was telling me that after I suffered a while (and I was suffering that day), He would establish me in a good job. I received that encouragement and began quietly to rejoice and thank Him for what I believed He was doing. However, in the middle of praising Him, the Lord spoke something challenging into my heart. He said, **"Do not send out any more resumes!"**

"Whaaa??? Don't send out any more resumes!" I said stunned and out loud. I had not expected to hear those words. In fact, just before I heard those words in my spirit, I had sat down at my computer with the intention of doing a bit of job hunting that afternoon. But in the next few minutes, I just sat there processing what I thought the Lord had said to me.

Faith to Find a Job

"How was I going to find a job, if I didn't send out any more resumes?" I thought to myself. I did not have any other interviews scheduled, and I was not aware of any *live* prospects on the horizon. Still, I knew...*I knew* I was hearing from God. Also, I knew that the Lord was waiting to see what I would do next. Would I cease from my works and **rest in my Faith** or would I pull up the Internet and continue *my works* as though *my effort* was my God?

I struggled for a moment, but then I turned off my computer, looked up to Heaven again, and said, *"Okay Lord...I trust you!"*

*"But You, O Lord, shall endure forever, and the remembrance of Your name to all generations. You will arise and have mercy on Zion; for **the time to favor her, Yes, the set time, has come**."*
(Psalm 102:12-14)

The very next day I got a call from a company that had been on my special list of organizations that I thought might be interested in someone with my qualifications. A job had been listed on their website, that had not been listed on the major job sites. In any case, several weeks before I got the call, I had filled out an online application that *included* all the dates related to my employment history. The bottom-line is, the call led to an interview and that interview led to *a job offer for a good job,* which I accepted! ***To God be all the Glory!***

"Blessed be the God and Father of our Lord Jesus Christ, who has blessed us with every spiritual blessing in the heavenly places in Christ.
"Therefore I also, after I heard of your faith in the Lord Jesus and your love for all the saints, do not cease to give thanks for you, making mention of you in my prayers: that the God of our

Faith to Find a Job

*Lord Jesus Christ, the Father of glory, may give to you the spirit of wisdom and revelation in the knowledge of Him, the eyes of your understanding being enlightened; that you may know what is the hope of His calling, what are the riches of the glory of His inheritance in the saints, and what is **the exceeding greatness of His power toward us who believe...**"*
(Ephesians 1: 3 and 15-19)

The exceeding greatness of His power *toward us who believe*...that is why I see the miraculous, supernatural power of God in my life. I am a believer in His exceeding great power. Make no mistake, that is what this book is about... putting your faith in God, who can open any door for you... who can create a job for you... who is bigger than you, and any circumstance! Nothing ...a prison record, a gap in your employment history, a lack of experience, a bad economy, a global pandemic, nothing, can stop God from providing you with a good job and the ability to be self-sufficient. A first-rate resume and knowing how to conduct a successful job search, will increase your faith that you will find a job. However, those things, no matter how excellent, have the power to make it happen. Humble yourself under the mighty hand of God *and rest* in the knowledge that the God you serve has the power to bless you with a good job.

*"Now to Him who is able to do exceedingly abundantly above all that we ask or think, according to the power that works in us, to Him be glory in the church by Christ Jesus to all generations, forever and ever. **Amen.**" (Ephesians 3:20-21)*

Faith to Find a Job

Conclusion

The Prayer of Prosperity

*"**For God is not unjust to forget your work and labor of love which you have shown toward His name**, in that you have ministered to the saints and do minister. And we, desire that each one of you show the same diligence to the full assurance of hope until the end, that you do not become sluggish, but imitate those who through faith and patience inherit the promises." (Hebrew 6:10)*

It has been my absolute joy to minister this word of hope to you! I can't tell you how excited I am for those of you who mix the words in this book with your faith. God is not unjust to forget your work and labor of love which you have shown toward His name....but through faith and patience **you will** inherit His promised blessings. You will find a good job! That is my confession of faith for you!

*"And the **LORD restored Job's losses when he prayed for his friends**. Indeed the LORD gave Job twice as much as he had before." (Job 42:10)*

Job 42:10 describes the ***Prayer of Prosperity***. Understand, Job had been struck by great adversity...he lost family, health and wealth. And like most of us when hard times came his way, Job looked inward, fell into a state of despair and cried out...'*Why me?*'

Toward the end of the story, however, Job receives a comforting word from the Lord. As a result, he is able to take his focus off himself and his problems, and he begins to pray for others. When he starts praying for others the Bible says,.. *"the LORD restored Job's losses when he prayed for his friends.*

If you need encouragement...encourage others. If you want to be appreciated...appreciate others. If you need forgiveness and grace...forgive others and deal graciously with those who offend you. If you need a job...pray for other people to get jobs. Take your focus off yourself...and what you need and pray for the economy, for the creation of jobs here in this nation and around the world. If you take that call seriously...as you pray for others around the world to prosper, God will prosper you.

"...knowing that whatever good anyone does, he will receive the same from the Lord...." (Ephesians 6:8)

God bless you!

Bibliography

Adams Media, *The Only Resume and Cover Letter Book You'll Ever Need*, F&W Publication Company, 2007

Hammond, Mac, *God's Waiting Room (*Cassette Series), Mac Hammond Ministries, Brooklyn Park, Minnesota

Krannich, Ronald I. and Banis, William J., Ph.ds, *High Impact Resume and Letters, How to Communicate Your Qualifications to Employers*, 8th Edition. Impact Publications, 1982,   1987, 1988, 1992, 1995, 1998, 2003

McVeigh, Kate, *The Favor Factor,* Harrison House, Tulsa, Oklahoma, January 1997

Meyers, Joyce, *Me and My Big Mouth*, Faithwords, Warners Books, Inc, New York, 1997

Moore, Keith, *The Significance of Saying (CD Series),* Moore Life Ministries, Branson,   Missouri, 2000

Osteen, Joel, *Increasing Favor (Cassette Series)*, Joel Osteen Ministries, Houston Texas

Resumes for Dummies, 4th Edition, Wiley Publishing Inc. 2002

Schuman, Nancy, *The Everything Resume Book*, 3rd Edition, Adams Media and F &W   Publication Company, 2008

Winston, Dr. Bill, *The Law of Confession, Revolutionize Your Life and Rewrite Your Future   With the Power of Words*, Harrison House, Tulsa, Oklahoma 2009

Faith to Find a Job

About the Author: L.C. Brown-Bush is an accomplished resume writer and employment minister who has for many years enjoyed helping people develop effective employment documents and smart strategies for conducting a job search. A spirit-filled Christian and passionate student of the Bible for more than two decades, **Faith to Find a Job** is her personal testimony of triumph and faith.